Introducing

READING

Florence Davies

Series Editors:
Ronald Carter and David Nunan

PENGUIN
ENGLISH

PENGUIN ENGLISH

Published by the Penguin Group
Penguin Books Ltd, 27 Wrights Lane, London W8 5TZ, England
Penguin Books USA Inc., 375 Hudson Street, New York, New York 10014, USA
Penguin Books Australia Ltd, Ringwood, Victoria, Australia
Penguin Books Canada Ltd, 10 Alcorn Avenue, Toronto, Ontario, Canada M4V 3B2
Penguin Books (NZ) Ltd, 182–190 Wairau Road, Auckland 10, New Zealand

Penguin Books Ltd, Registered Offices: Harmondsworth, Middlesex, England

First published 1995
1 3 5 7 9 10 8 6 4 2

Illustrations by Nigel Andrews

Typeset by Datix International Limited, Bungay, Suffolk
Printed in England by Clays Ltd, St Ives plc
Filmset in 10/13 pt Monophoto Times

The insights provided by work in applied linguistics can be of genuine support to all teachers facing the many complex demands of language learning and teaching. The Penguin English *Introducing Applied Linguistics* series aims to provide short, clear and accessible guides to key topics – helping teachers to keep abreast of this rapidly developing field by explaining recent research and its relevance to common problems and concerns. The books are designed for practical use: they focus on recognizable classroom contexts, suggest problem-solving approaches, and include activities and questions for further study.

Introducing Applied Linguistics presumes an increasing convergence of interest among all English language teachers, and it aims to be relevant both to teachers of English as a second or foreign language and to teachers of English as a mother tongue. As the relationship between linguistics and language teaching continues to develop, so the need grows for books which introduce the field. This series has been developed to meet that need.

The words that appear in **bold** type are explained
in the glossary.

Acknowledgements

The publishers make grateful acknowledgement to the following for permission to reproduce copyright material: *In the Know: A Guide to English and the National Curriculum*, edited by J. Harris and J. Wilkinson, Stanley Thornes, 1990; *Reading for Learning in the Sciences*, by F. Davies and T. Green, Oliver and Boyd, 1984; *Reading for Professional Purposes: Methods and Materials in Teaching Languages*, by F. Davies, first published by Uitgeverij Acco Leuven/Amersfoort, 1985; *Cohesion in English*, by M. A. K. Halliday and P. Hasan, Longman, 1976; *On the Surface of Discourse*, by M. Hoey, Allen and Unwin, 1983; *Conversational Investigations of Reading*, by S. Harri-Augstein and L. Thomas, from *Reading in a Foreign Language*, by J. C. Alderson and A. H. Urquhart, Longman, 1984; *Reading and Learning*, by N. Hedge, unpublished Ph.D. thesis, University of Liverpool, 1991; *Language of the Inner City*, by W. Labov, Basil Blackwell Ltd, 1972; *Undergraduate Prospectus*, Liverpool University, 1991; extracts from project material, L. I. N. C., 1992; *Learning from the Written Word*, by E. Lunzer, K. Gardener, F. Davies and T. Greene, Oliver and Boyd, 1984; *Learning to Learn from Text*, by A. Morris and N. Stewart-Dore, Addison–Wesley, 1984; *Toward an Integrated Model of Reading*, by D. Rumelhart, from *Attention and Performance IV*, edited by S. Dornic, Lawrence Erlbaum, 1977; *Understanding Understanding*, by D. Rumelhart, from *Understanding Reading Comprehension*, edited by J. Flood, International Reading Association, 1984; *Study Geography Stage 1*, by Rushby et al, Longman, 1975.

Every effort has been made to trace copyright holders in every case. The publishers would be interested to hear from any not acknowledged here.

For a full list of references, please see page 177.

Contents

Contents

Contents

Contents

Introduction

Reading is a complex process which, since the turn of the century, has been extensively studied across a wide range of different disciplines. This is manifestly reflected in the vast literature on reading and on the teaching of reading in the contexts of both mother tongue and foreign language classrooms. This book is addressed to teachers from both of these contexts; as it is an introductory text, however, the ground covered has had to be limited. None the less my aim in the book has been to focus on aspects of reading which I believe have received less attention to date than they deserve.

Thus the aspects of reading and the teaching of reading which receive the greatest emphasis in the book and which represent the central, recurring, strands of the book are: individual readers engaging in various kinds of reading tasks in the real world, the social contexts in which such readers engage (or not) and interact (in some way) with texts, and the nature and variety of texts and their role as 'participants' in the interaction between reader and writer.

In this central concern with socializing and humanizing reading and the teaching of reading, however, I have also been concerned that such an emphasis should be supported by evidence. Thus the book introduces readers to a wide range of both formal and informal methods and criteria for studying reading behaviour, for evaluating current 'models' of reading, for describing and analysing different types of text and for designing a reading programme in different classroom contexts. These four aspects of reading are represented in the four chapters of the book.

If readers make 'discoveries' during the course of reading the book, these will surely not equal those which I have made from discussions with colleagues, particularly with Nicki Hedge, Mike Scott, and Wendy Knight-Garcia, with students too numerous to name, and from my interactions with the writers of the texts on which I have drawn. To all of these people I am indebted, but most of all to the students, who were always so willing to talk about their own experiences of reading.

1 Studying reading behaviour

Reading is private. It is a mental, or cognitive, process which involves a reader in trying to follow and respond to a message from a writer who is distant in space and time. Because of this privacy, the process of reading and responding to a writer is not directly observable.

However, as teachers we are required to make some attempt to understand this process and to find ways of observing it. This chapter introduces a range of different procedures for studying reading behaviour. It focuses first on informal methods for investigating personal reading outside the classroom and then outlines a range of more formal methods for studying reading in the classroom.

1.1 Informal studies of personal reading outside the classroom

The aim of informal studies is threefold: first to gain some understanding of the ways in which individual readers perceive reading, secondly to provide a real-world context for the reading undertaken in the classroom and thirdly to initiate a dialogue with students as a means of encouraging them to reflect on the nature and purposes of their own reading.

Informal studies of individual readers (or small groups of readers) can be based on interviews, questionnaires, or reading diaries, and ideally should be undertaken at regular intervals throughout the school year. In second language (L2) contexts, readers will need to be encouraged to consider their first language (L1) reading first and then their L2 reading. The broad questions such studies aim to explore are as follows:

— what is the reading material that different readers are required to read in everyday life or that they choose to read for various purposes (for example, for day-to-day survival, for general interest, for personal interest, for social purposes, for pleasure and aesthetic appreciation and for academic purposes) and what is the range of different types of text that are read?

— what features of text are of importance to different readers?

— to what extent do social, **affective** or cultural factors influence readers' responses to different types of text and to reading?

— how do different readers evaluate their own competence as readers?

— what **strategies** do readers report using when encountering difficulties in reading?

It is such questions that have guided my own informal studies of individual readers in the course of writing this book. The readers in my sample are varied, ranging from a 2-year-old beginning to acquire a concept of reading, to advanced adults, typically teachers following a postgraduate course of studies, and reading in either L1 or L2.

Not surprisingly the answers to the questions I explored are very varied.

1.1.1 Reading materials selected by different readers

The range of different texts to which readers are exposed in real life is extensive. Even a pre-reader, Philip, at 2 years of age, is already demonstrating an interest in a range of different types of text: explanatory/informative books, narrative texts, reports of everyday experiences and rhymes.

Naturally the range of texts read by adult readers and the

purposes for reading is substantially greater and confirms Halliday's (1985/89) observation that real-world reading can often involve the processing of over twenty distinct types of written material during the course of a single week. For the adult readers in my study, the different types of text read over a period of a fortnight included predictable 'genres' such as newspapers, academic texts and novels, etc, but also less predictable material such as student essays, poll tax instructions, job applications, messages from gas or electricity board officials, CD covers, religious music, knitting patterns and product descriptions.

The picture of text selection from junior and secondary school readers presents a much more diverse range of preferences and reading practices. For many of these readers the survival reading obligatory for many adults is still avoidable and it would appear that individual readers are free to restrict their reading to a relatively narrow range of different types of text. In addition gender differences in text preferences reported by Whitehead *et al.* (1977), Heather (1981), Gorman *et al.* (1981, 1982) and Ingham (1981) appear to operate, with girls tending to express a preference for fiction and boys being more likely to include non-fiction in their selections of text.

For example, Helen's selection of texts at 8 years of age is mainstream modern fiction with an orientation towards humour and slightly bizarre plots, rather than pure fantasy and poetry. She also reports enjoying rereading certain books introduced to her by her mother. However, her reading of non-fiction is restricted to the instructions for computer games, which she finds very difficult, and some 'facts' books for topic work.

By contrast William, at 10 years of age, selects from a wide range of non-fiction and fiction. His favourite texts include an encyclopedia-type informative book, single-topic 'information' series, classic and modern detective stories, newspapers, particularly special sports editions, a software computer magazine, comics, promotions printed on computer games' boxes in shops, catalogues and instruction manuals for computer games. Thus William's selection contrasts sharply with Helen's more literary, personal selections.

John's preferences, at 14 years of age, are approaching those of the adults in my sample, in that there is some 'survival' reading, for example, reading instructions for car waxing and cooking Chicken Kiev, but there is also evidence that he is choosing, almost deliberating, to restrict the range of types of text he is willing to read. Thus amongst the texts he discusses are a sports magazine, a newspaper, a leaflet on AIDS, signs in the supermarket, advertisements, a trade magazine; letters relating to school trips and a club, an April Fools' letter and 'school' reading: Shakespeare and modern fiction.

From these brief examples drawn from my studies there is some indication of the very wide range of different types of reading material read outside the classroom. Even within a single age group, this reflects a variety well beyond that encountered in most classroom or course books. Not only is there a wide range of materials but all are examples of texts which in L2 contexts are typically described as being **authentic**, or, in L1 contexts, as **real**. Here authentic or real texts are defined as texts selected by a reader or a teacher that are recognized by the reader as <u>meeting some need</u> for information, entertainment, aesthetic satisfaction or instruction, in which aspects and patterns of language are learned within a meaningful context.

In L2 contexts, authentic material is contrasted with simplified material and in L1 with **structured reading schemes**. These are texts selected by a textbook writer or teacher for the purpose of <u>teaching</u> a preselected item or aspect of language, for example, phonic rules, the shape of a word, a linguistic structure, where context is strictly controlled in order to focus attention on the feature of language being taught.

In view of the difference between texts selected for reading outside the classroom and also within the classroom, we should consider:

— what might be the advantages and disadvantages of using authentic or simplified texts in the classroom?

— how might readers selecting from a limited range of texts be encouraged to read more widely?

— is there a place in the curriculum for the study of materials students read outside the classroom?

These issues are explored in chapter 4; for further reading see Exton and O'Rourke (1993), Johns and Davies (1983), Taylor (1990), Wallace (1992).

1.1.2 Social, affective and cultural factors

For all readers, the experience of reading provides an opportunity to explore and relate to a wider world than one's own. In this sense reading extends social, cultural and academic horizons, and is in part determined by, and gives rise to, affective responses to text as the reader interacts with the writer. At the same time, the evidence from my readers suggests that reading contributes both positively and negatively to the growth of the reader's self-concept.

Thus for Helen, her reading of fiction allows her to identify with certain <u>role models</u>, for example Princess Florizella, whom she admires for her qualities of independence and non-conformism: 'Well ... she wants to do things that everybody else would not dream of doing ... without getting told off'. For William, his organized approach to reading is increasingly shaped by his perception of himself as a discriminating consumer of a wide range of publications. In this role it seems that the external world in which William explores and purchases books is an important part of his reading environment. Introducing me to his computer magazine, he reports: 'I bought this on its first issue and I've been buying it ever since and it tells you about lots of events and things and games and charts and diary dates.' Of *Arms and Armour*, he tells me that there are certain shops 'which always seem to have it ... You go down and right on the corner there's this newsagent and I used to go in there, find it, pay my money and come out reading it ... and I would flick through and read it all the way until I got home.'

By contrast, John appears to be at a transition phase in establishing his identity as a reader. On the one hand, he is at pains to distance himself from the role of 'reader of fiction'. 'I enjoy reading to find out about things, but novels ... not really.' On the other hand, his capacity for engagement with literature is evident: 'I read *The Woman in Black* by Susan Hill. It was very good. I really enjoyed that.' With his friends he talks about 'everyday life rather than books and things ... sport and things'.

Stuart, a craft apprentice aged 17, expresses most explicitly his virtual rejection of the role of 'reader': 'I don't read any books that are well-known for their educational value or because they are reputed to be good. I read mainly books that are scandalous or violent; perhaps this could stem from our daily order of newspapers [*Sun, News of the World*] renowned not to include educational or well-written news ... It could also stem from schools, the old phobia of friends saying "poof" or calling bookworms "crawlers".'

The role of cultural factors is also reported by advanced adults reading in L2: 'perhaps my understanding was a culture difference ... maybe I had ... a conception that was a misconception.'

From reports such as those above it would appear that social, affective and cultural factors play a major role in influencing readers' selection of texts, their interaction with text and their concepts of themselves as readers or non-readers. As teachers we should consider ways in which we can encourage positive attitudes to reading while at the same time recognizing and respecting individual differences. We should also consider whether or not there is a place in the reading programme for the discussion of affective and cultural responses to text. These issues are explored further in chapter 4.

1.1.3 Criteria for text selection and important features of text

The features of text to which different readers respond clearly play an important part in learning from text, whether such learning is about language or about the world.

For 2-year-old Philip, the illustrations and visual features of the text are clearly of paramount importance, but there are other features of texts which he is increasingly attending to as a result of his experience of 'shared reading' (Carter 1990 and ms., Meek 1988, 1990). These include a number of the steps in the learning-to-read sequence first observed by Marie Clay (1969) in her study of the weekly reading of 100 readers in their first year of schooling. In brief these involve: page matching, wherein the message of the page is memorized without locating any detail in the print, line matching, locating some words within a memorized line, reading the spaces and coordinating visually recognized word patterns with speech patterns and the spaces between words. However, Philip will need more experience of shared reading before he will take the next steps towards real reading, that is, paying increasing attention to the relationship between visual and spelling patterns and their spoken forms and monitoring the match between written and spoken words in order to self-correct.

In this learning Philip's progress is clearly facilitated by the predictability of familiar stories, and texts which have been read and reread. However, for 8-year-old Helen, predictability is a negative, not a positive, feature of a story; thus Nina Bawden's *The Peppermint Pig* is approved because 'it gives quite a few surprises'. In addition, credibility is important: about *Almost Goodbye Guzzler* by Helen Cresswell and Judy Brown she remarks: 'it's only the bit about the genie which couldn't happen in real life'.

The importance of <u>visuals</u> is reported by readers from the complete range of ages and reading contexts. Thus Anna, aged 7, is strongly interested in layout as well as illustrations: 'At the front there's some pictures and at the back there's exactly the same pictures.'

John is also clearly sensitive to the impact of visual presentation. It was this, and also his interest in the topic, which drew his attention to an AIDS leaflet: 'There was a leaflet on AIDS that came through the door and it was black and it had a big thing saying AIDS . . . It sort of hit you.' Clearly the content was also of interest: 'I read that . . . and it was quite . . . um . . . relevant to everyday life and quite worrying.'

Predictably, highly efficient adult readers report on paying attention to <u>textual supports</u>, such as tables, indices, appendices, quotations and footnotes.

ACTIVITY

From the above it is clear that the features of text to which readers pay attention may not be those to which attention is drawn in the classroom or in course books. Consider what features of text you pay particular attention to. Could you be a more effective reader by directing attention to other features? Is there a place in the classroom for close examination of different features of text, particularly the features adults reported paying attention to?

1.1.4 Readers' evaluation of their reading competence

My studies indicate that while less experienced readers are capable of analysing their own reading weaknesses, they are more likely to evaluate themselves positively as readers than the advanced adults who not only expressed doubts about their competence as readers but frequently reported 'breakdown' in the process of reading: 'I'm amazed that I've had a complete blank ... It's worrying ... Looking at it again ... paragraph is just a string of jargon ... nothing my memory can relate to, I'm just rejecting it totally.'

Other (advanced) readers confessed to not enjoying reading: Koto, a Japanese teacher/administrator (who is in practice highly successful as a reader of English as a foreign language), responded: 'Reading is usually a tiring activity to me because I haven't established a reading habit [in Japanese] in my childhood. I am more sensitive to visual things and I tend to rely on them ... if the reading involves a conceptual or abstract subject ... it's difficult/impossible to draw a mental picture or image. My concentration is always distracted by the "idea" of reading, namely there is another Koto shouting "You have to concentrate: Read!", and he interrupts me further.'

By contrast Inas, a university teacher from Egypt, is enthusiastic, though realistic, about her reading: 'I love reading. Sometimes I feel I am a good reader when I feel I understand a good deal of what I am reading and I've managed to read at a good pace. Other times, especially when I lose my concentration and aim for reading, I feel I am a bad reader.'

From the above there is evidence that even for advanced academic readers following a postgraduate course of study, reading is not simple and not without difficulties. It seems that if readers are to learn from text, there is no avoiding hard labour. This is a point which is frequently ignored in many course books, but which is supported by the evidence from extensive research on reading reported in chapter 2.

1.1.5 The strategies readers report using

If most of the readers in the sample reported having difficulties with reading, many also recognized that the hard work of reading can be facilitated by the adoption of certain strategies. In coping with the demand of difficult texts, readers reported engaging in different kinds of reading: skimming, scanning, skipping and slow, careful study reading. They also reported using a variety of different strategies: regression and rereading; reading aloud; use of context to infer the meaning of unknown words; the formulation of questions; a preliminary review and analysis of the reading task; use of background information; underlining and colour coding; monitoring one's reading pace; and checking and revising initial interpretations. It is with more formal investigations of such reading behaviours that the following sections are concerned.

1.2   Studying reading behaviour in the classroom

In this more public context of the classroom or test situation, the focus is on what readers do when they are engaged in the process of reading or are required to produce an outcome or product of reading, for instance completing a test of performance such as a comprehension test.

The methods introduced in this section include methods for observing and analysing both reading aloud and silent reading and are methods which have traditionally been used by teachers and/or researchers for one or more of the following purposes:

— as a means of giving students 'practice' in reading;
— as the basis of tests or measures of performance;
— as the basis for diagnosing and helping individual readers;
— as the basis for investigating research questions about the reading process.

1.2.1   Studying oral reading behaviour

Oral reading as reading practice

There is little doubt that across cultures and throughout history the most visible evidence of reading behaviour is oral reading, that is, reading aloud. When we listen to a reader reading a text aloud we can 'see and hear' the extent to which the oral reading matches the written text. It is thus not surprising that in the beginning reading classroom, in both L1 and L2, reading aloud is an important method for giving learners reading practice. However, it must be noted that researchers such as Southgate and Arnold (1981) present evidence to suggest that it should not be a predominant form of practice.

Oral reading as a measure of reading performance and progress

In addition to being a means of practising reading, oral reading has traditionally also been the basis of both informal and standardized tests of reading performance. Standardized tests are tests that have been developed through extensive statistical analysis of items used to measure performance and that demonstrate **reliability** and **validity**. Many teachers will have some experience of using standardized tests, either through involvement in a monitoring programme implemented by the school, local authority, or a government department, or as part of one of the many language proficiency tests that are used in the teaching of EFL/EAP.

Oral reading as the basis for diagnosing reading behaviour

In the classroom, oral reading is also widely used as a diagnostic tool. By listening to individual readers, teachers gain valuable information about how individual readers are approaching a text and about the strategies they use when confronted with difficulties. In the one-to-one situation they can initiate a dialogue about the text and about the learner's response to the text and the task, help the reader correct errors and provide guidance. Such guidance is based on the teacher's observation and analysis of what the reader is doing – how he or she is making sense of the print. In listening to reading aloud there is much to observe and analyse.

ACTIVITY

Consider beginning readers in either L1 or L2, reading a text in which there is a percentage (for example, 10 per cent) of words or structures new to the reader and requiring effort to **decode**. Try to predict the different behaviours you might be able to observe or to record as you listen to the reading with a copy of the text in front of you. Does the reader appear confident and fluent or hesitant and uncertain? When and what kind of errors are made? What strategies are used when the reader meets a new word or structure? Is the reader conscious of making errors?

A range of different behaviours in oral reading

When we listen to and observe oral reading we quickly see that there is a great deal 'going on'; indeed so much that it is difficult to record all of the observable behaviours that are manifest. These include the relative speed and fluency of the reading, the degree of confidence or anxiety exhibited by the reader, the use of different strategies, such as following the words or lines with a finger, **regression** to an earlier part of the text, or reference forward to a part of the text not read, hesitation and self-correction. In addition, with careful observation it is possible to note the number of times and the places in the text where the reader makes an error, or miscue, and whether the error is an omission, a mispronunciation or a **substitution**. In the classroom, the observation and recording of such behaviours provide the basis for drawing up individual profiles of readers which can be analysed for diagnostic purposes.

Recording and analysing oral reading for diagnostic purposes

Increasingly, the observation, recording and analysis of oral reading in the classroom is also informed by the findings of research studies of **miscue analysis** pioneered by teacher-researchers such as Marie Clay (1968, 1969), Kenneth Goodman (1969) and Rose-Marie Weber (1970). For such researchers, miscue analysis involves the systematic recording and analysis of errors as a source of information about how readers are processing text. It is based on the assumption that errors are 'informative', and that from them, we can learn something about the knowledge sources the reader is bringing to the reading of a text.

For instance, in a pioneering study undertaken in New Zealand, Clay recorded and analysed the reading errors of 100 5-year-olds weekly over the period of their first year of schooling. From her analysis of 10,525 errors, Clay provided evidence that these young readers were using their knowledge of the grammar of their native language to make predictions about the identity of new words. When they produced substitutions, 72 per cent were found to be of the same **word class**, for example, noun, verb, or adjective as the original; in addition, with increasing confidence there was an increase in the number of **self-corrections**. Such findings have provided a basis for the development of procedures for analysing oral reading in the classroom, which are now widely used by teachers in both L1 and L2.

Oral reading for diagnostic purposes as a supplement to standardized tests

The analysis of miscues as a diagnostic procedure is not regarded as an alternative to standardized performance measures, but as an essential supplement. As Marie Clay observes, performance measures are necessary, but do not provide a basis on which to design a reading programme, or on which to provide help for individual readers.

Clay contrasts observation with traditional testing:

Educators have relied on systematic testing rather than systematic observation of learning. An undue focus on testing can deprive teachers and administrators of valuable information about learners and their learning . . . I am certain that in education, evaluation needs to pay more attention to the systematic observation of learners who are on their way to . . . final assessments. (Clay 1979/1992:1)

In her Reading Recovery Programme, recently introduced as the basis of a remediation programme in a number of LEAs in Britain, Clay presents an empirically tested system of observation which involves teachers in keeping a running record of their young readers. A central feature of this record is the analysis of the miscues readers make when reading aloud. While many teachers will not be in a position to implement Clay's Reading Recovery Programme, the miscue analysis methodology can be implemented in any educational context and has been widely adopted in L1 and L2 classrooms.

The basic of miscue analysis

As we have seen, the basis of miscue analysis is the classification of 'errors' or miscues made in reading aloud, with reference to observable reading behaviour, for example:
— omission of word or phrase

— rereading/repeating
— self-correcting
— segmentation of word(s)
— reference to illustration
— substitution of word(s)

and/or the type of 'cue' or information source used when producing a substitution, for example:

— substitution in the same grammatical class as the original, or not;
— substitution that is semantically acceptable, that is, preserves the meaning of the original, or not;
— substitution that is orthographically similar to the original or not;
— substitution that has a similar sound, or phonology, to the original.

From an analysis of this kind, it is possible for the teacher to gain some understanding of the strategies readers use for decoding text, and of the sources of information upon which readers may draw. When readers make more or less informed guesses or **hypotheses** about missing words, or when miscues occur, we can see to some extent which sources of information are being utilized and which are not. For example, some readers may show a pattern of relying more heavily on semantic information and failing to check letter–sound correspondences; others, particularly in ESL (English as a Second Language) and EFL (English as a Foreign Language), may be making incorrect syntactic predictions, drawing upon knowledge of their first language; others may be focusing almost exclusively on letter–sound correspondence and ignoring meaning as a check.

With information from such analyses teachers are then in a position to help the learner make more effective use of different sources of information, particularly those to which they are paying less attention. It is thus not surprising that miscue analysis has been widely used in both L1 and ESL/EFL classrooms and research studies.

Procedures for recording miscues

The procedures for recording and analysing miscues vary according to educational context. However, the principles of recording are basically simple and teachers can modify or refine the procedures they use for recording in response to what they learn about their own students' reading behaviour and needs.

The procedures all involve:
— the selection of a text of at least 300 words that 'stretches' the reader, one that will present some decoding challenges to the reader, and hence will generate errors;
— the copying of the text to be read as the basis for the teacher's record;
— the use of some kind of 'coding' system for recording errors;
— ideally the use of a tape-recorder to record the interview;
— the silent reading of the text by the student, followed by a discussion of the text with the teacher/observer;
— the reading aloud of the text by the student without 'corrective' intervention by the teacher/researcher;
— a follow-up discussion of the text with the teacher/observer;
— the subsequent analysis of the record using a marking key or code.

An example of a well-established marking code developed by the Language in the National Curriculum (LINC) team is presented in the table on page 17.

ACTIVITY

Two examples of the miscues of different students reading the same text, taken from the Neale Analysis of Reading Skills (1958), are presented on pages 18 and 19. Study the coding of the errors and the marking key to be sure that you can classify each type of miscue.

When you have classified all of the errors, work with a colleague and try to answer the following questions:

THE CODING SYMBOLS: A MARKING KEY

(1) substitution	— the word substituted is written above the corresponding word in the text,
	e.g. When Then Mother Tortoise began to look into the picnic baskets.
(2) self-correction	— the miscue is written above the word in the text and is marked as shown,
	e.g. They picked up the sandwiches, but just as they were going to eat them, a little voice said, 'Aha! I knew you'd cheat.'
(3) repetition	— the words repeated are underlined. Double underlining indicates words have been repeated twice,
	e.g. 'It's six years now,' said Mother Tortoise 'He ought to be back by now.'
(4) omission	— the word omitted is circled in the text,
	e.g. So they waited (and) another year passed, and another, and they got ravenous.
(5) insertion	— the inserted word is written above an insertion mark,
	e.g. And in three years they reached the picnic place.
(6) reversal	— (there is no example of this in the marked text shown but) the words reversed are marked with a continuous line,
	e.g. 'yes, I suppose he ought,' said Father
(7) hesitation	— an oblique stroke is marked before the word paused at,
	e.g. 'Well, do you/swear, do you promise faithfully,' said the baby, 'that you won't touch a thing till I come back?'
(8) long pause, teacher gives help	— the world given is written above the text and marked by T,
	e.g. So they waited and another year passed, and another, and they got ravens ravenous. T

(numbers refer to those in the marked text)

— which miscues are semantically acceptable, that is, very similar in meaning to the original words or to the text as a whole?

— which miscues reveal the effective use of grapho-phonic cues?

— which miscues suggest an over-reliance on grapho-phonic cues or confusion arising from different pronunciations of certain letters?

— which miscues are syntactically acceptable in that they are the same class of word as the original, for example, noun, verb, adjective etc?

1a

The lions / final act was in progress. *[f-i ©]*

Jack / stood waiting to clear the ring. *[s-e] [call]*

Tonight the thunder outside the circus *[third] [was]*

tent had made the lions restless.

Suddenly Tess the lion trainer *[turned]*

stumbled. Her whip fell. The youngest *[fall]*

lion sprang towards her. Swiftly

Jack leaped inside the cage,

cracking the whip with great skill.

His prompt action enabled Tess to *[prompet akton] [R]*

regain control very quickly. During that *[range] [countrily-conscious] [quick] [quickly] [hollowed]*

brief adventure, however, Jack had

decided upon his future work. *[discovered] [frontier]*

(Author's data)

—which miscues are not of the same class as the original but are an acceptable alternative?
—which miscues suggest that the student is monitoring his or her reading effectively?
—which miscues indicate a breakdown of confidence?

1b

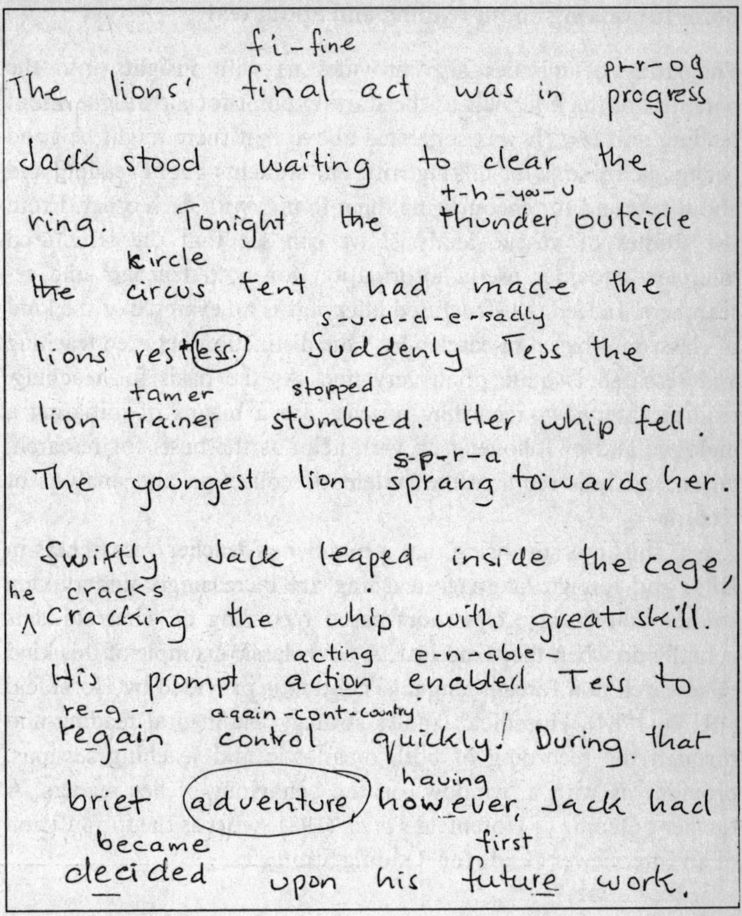

The lions' final act was in progress
(fi-fine above "final"; p-r-og above "progress")

Jack stood waiting to clear the

ring. Tonight the thunder outside
(t-h-yoo-u above "thunder")

the circus tent had made the
(kircle above "circus")

lions restless. Suddenly Tess the
("restless" has "ess." circled; s-u-d-d-e-sadly above "Suddenly")

lion trainer stumbled. Her whip fell.
(tamer above "trainer"; stopped above "stumbled")

The youngest lion sprang towards her.
(s-p-r-a above "sprang")

Swiftly Jack leaped inside the cage,

cracking the whip with great skill.
(he cracks above, with caret ^ before "cracking")

His prompt action enabled Tess to
(acting above "action"; e-n-able- above "enabled")

regain control quickly! During that
(re-g-- above "regain"; again-cont-country above "control")

brief adventure however, Jack had
("adventure" circled; having above "however")

decided upon his future work.
(became above "decided"; first above "future"; "future" underlined)

(Author's data)

—which miscues suggest a 'gap' in the student's vocabulary?

Your answers to these questions should provide the basis for considering how you could help the readers become more effective.

Miscue analysis and the structured interview as a starting point for talking about reading and about text

The study of miscues also provides us with insights into the potential of the interview as the starting point for a dialogue about reading and text. It was suggested above that there might be good pedagogic reasons for talking with our students about reading and about text and for encouraging them to talk with each other. From the studies of miscue analysis, we can see that the structured interview provides useful information for both teachers and researchers. Indeed the structured interview is an example of the kind of classroom-based research where the distinction between teaching and research is quite often very fine. As the basis for teaching, reading interviews recording miscues are a means of initiating a dialogue and of following up with help; as the basis for research, miscue analysis requires the systematic collection and analysis of records.

It is thus not surprising that a number of teacher/researchers in EFL and foreign language teaching are increasingly undertaking studies that involve classroom-based recording of what students actually do when they read text. A now classic example of this kind of research in a foreign language context is provided by Hosenfeld (1977b, 1984). Hosenfeld studies strategy use in oral reading and through the recording of both diagnostic and teaching sessions, provides us with a 'window' on the behaviour of her readers. A further outcome of Hosenfeld's *et al.* (1981) work is the formulation of an Interviewer Guide for Reading Strategies.

Miscue analysis as the basis for a model of the reading process

As we shall see in chapter 2, data from miscue analysis has also provided the basis for the development of a 'psycholinguistic' model of reading by Goodman (1969, 1988), which has been widely influential in both L1 and L2 contexts.

1.2.2   Studying the outcomes of silent reading

Analysis of errors in the context of silent reading

However, it is not only in the context of oral reading that 'misreadings' are analysed. In one recent study of Bernhardt and Berkermeyer discussed in Bernhardt (1991), errors are drawn from the summaries students produced from their reading of texts in a foreign language. The texts on which the students based their summaries, or recalls, were examples of authentic reading material: a business letter and different types of newspaper reports (albeit typically from popular, rather than quality papers).

In this study errors are categorized with reference to broad linguistic and conceptual criteria. Thus the categories Bernhardt uses for her analyses are:

— word recognition errors, for example, interpreting the German word for 'acquaintances' as 'relatives';

— phonemic/graphemic errors, for example, misinterpreting a word on the basis of similarity, but not identity, or orthographic or phonemic features, for example, *streben* = striving, as *sterben* = dying;

— syntactic errors include interpreting the present tense as the past, or a singular for a plural etc;

— intratextual perception errors; for example, failing to recognize, or misinterpreting the type of text and/or its communicative purpose; for example, as in assuming a letter is a personal letter when it is a business letter;

— metacognitive errors: the expression, through question marks, annotation etc of uncertainty about how to interpret the text;

— errors in the application of prior knowledge: the inappropriate use of prior knowledge or of doubtful information.

From this we can see that the sources of information upon which Bernhardt's analysis is based are very similar to those identified in studies of oral reading. This suggests that Bernhardt's methodology may have potential for teachers working with more advanced students and particularly for teachers who are constrained by the problems of large classes. For Bernhardt the methodology is seen to have the advantages of relative ease of collecting data, efficient use of time, the possibility of eliciting data from large classes, and collection under different conditions.

THE STUDY AS THE BASIS OF A MODEL OF READING

Bernhardt's study also represents one approach to analysis that aims to understand the complex processes involved in reading for comprehension. As such it forms the basis of her 'developmental' model of reading (Bernhardt 1991). However, Bernhardt does not discuss the teaching implications of her methodology in any depth nor the potential of using the analysis of recall '**protocols**' as a starting point for initiating classroom discussion about reading and text.

Analysing the outcomes of silent reading: comprehension exercises and tests

Unlike oral reading, silent reading is not open to direct observation. For this reason the traditional means of developing or studying silent reading has been to give readers tasks that require them to produce an outcome of reading, such as a judgement of some kind. In the context of teaching and in many research contexts, the most widely used outcome has been the comprehension exercise or test, or the multiple-choice test.

Typically, the comprehension exercise involves the selection of a relatively short, isolated extract from an authentic text, or the construction of a text for the purposes of the test, and the design of a series of questions that may be more or less open or closed, and more or less literal and inferential (Bloom 1965) but frequently requiring relatively short answers. Even shorter answers are elicited in multiple-choice formats.

COMPREHENSION EXERCISES AS PRACTICE IN DEVELOPING READING SKILLS

Traditionally in the context of primary, secondary and higher education, in both L1 and L2 contexts, the comprehension exercise has been the principal method for developing and practising reading skills once basic decoding skills are acquired. Indeed evidence from surveys such as those undertaken by Durkin (1978) in the US, and Lunzer and Gardner (1979) in the UK indicate that until recently, the comprehension exercise was almost the only type of activity used for the development of **higher-order reading skills**. However, as Davies and Greene (1982) demonstrate, the comprehension exercise has serious limitations as a means of encouraging learning, a point to which we return below and in chapter 4 where a range of alternatives is introduced.

COMPREHENSION TESTS AS MEASURES OF PERFORMANCE

Just as oral reading has been the basis of standardized measures of performance, so too has the comprehension test or its variants traditionally been the basis for both informal classroom-based and standardized measures of performance. In view of the widespread use of such tests and our inevitable familiarity with them, it will be useful at this stage to evaluate an informal comprehension exercise.

ACTIVITY

In order to do this, you are asked here to undertake a typical comprehension exercise based on text 1c. In addition, you are asked to try and monitor the process you go through as you find the answers to the questions. So in doing the exercise, you are asked to follow the procedure below:
1. Skim-read the text and then try to answer the skim-read questions on pages 26–7.

2. Then study the comprehension questions that follow and see if you can answer any of them without going back to the text. Write your answers in and mark them NT.
3. Next, try to find the answers for which you need to study the text.
4. As you try to find the answer, put a circle around any parts of the text that you think will help you find it.
5. Put a double circle around the part that you are sure gives you the answer.
6. Write your answer in the space provided.

When you have completed the questions:

1. Reread the text and underline any parts you did not understand.
2. Write down any important questions in relation to the text that you would like answers to.
3. Now write a summary of the text.

1c

Reading comprehension is usually measured by means of retrieval rate from memory. Despite its virtues, such a method suffers at least from one shortcoming. It can be argued that retrieval is the final link in the act of text processing, and therefore the earlier phases of the process ought to deserve more attention from researchers (see e.g. Kieras and Just, 1984). The experiment reported here combines on-line and off-line methods in order to study reading comprehension and learning. It examines the comprehension and learning of coherent and incoherent texts as reflected by eye movement patterns and recall peformance produced by the same subjects. Coherence is defined at the textual macrolevel as the reorganization of a text under a structural schema or script. Macrolevel coherence can be distin-guished from microlevel coherence (see van Dijk and Kintsch, 1983). At a textual microlevel, coherence can be defined as 'cohesion' (see Halliday and Hasan, 1976) or 'argument overlap' (see Kintsch and van Dijk, 1978), in which case coherence means that two consecutive sentences are connected with each other with a referential tie. The present experiment emphasizes macro-structural coherence.

Semantic and schematic structures of texts play an important control function both in text comprehension and production (see e.g. Kintsch and van Dijk, 1978). This notion is supported by evidence from two lines of research. Firstly, there are several relevant studies of memory recall (e.g. Kintsch and Yarbrough, 1982; Mandler and Johnson, 1977; Meyer, 1977; Stein and Glenn, 1979; Thorndyke, 1977). Secondly, on-line recordings such as eye movements have provided corroborating evidence (Blanchard and Iran-Nejad, 1987; Dee-Lucas, Just, Carpenter and Daneman, 1982; Shebilske and Fisher, 1983). Studies that would explicitly combine these two approaches are lacking so far.

Research on learning and recall of both narrative (e.g. Kintsch and Greene, 1978; Mandler and Johnson, 1977; Thorndyke, 1977) and expository texts (e.g. Kieras, 1978; Kintsch and Yarbrough, 1982; Vauras, von Wright and Kinnunen 1991) has shown that logical, coherent and conventionally organized texts activate adequate schema-based expectations that can effectively be used in interpreting, constructing and recalling textual information. If the text is incoherent to the extent that it violates these schema-based expectations, the reconstruction of the information is more difficult, resulting in a poor recall peformance (e.g. Kieras, 1978; Kintsch and Yarbrough, 1982; Vauras, von Wright and Kinnunen, 1991). However, even in the latter case the structural schemata are effective tools in making it possible for readers to comprehend ill-structured texts by reconstruction (e.g. Kintsch, Mandel and Kozminsky, 1977; Stein, 1979).

A hierarchic organization of a text is known especially to affect readers' selection strategies. When an expository text is organized in terms of explicit hierarchic levels, a 'levels effect' is usually found: propositions from the higher levels of the text hierarchy are much better recalled than propositions low in the hierarchy (e.g. Kintsch, Kozminsky, Streby, McKoon and Keenan, 1975; Meyer, 1977; Meyer, Brandt and Bluth, 1980). However, with complex expository *texts the levels effect is more intricate than with narratives, leading to somewhat equivocal results. The levels effect may not be found at all when the lower-level propositions have tight logical ties, e.g. in terms of cause and effect (Dunn, Matthews and Bieger, 1982; c.f. also Vauras, von Wright and Kinnunen, 1991), or when the text passages are complicated, organized around several topics (Kieras, 1981).*

In spite of their general usefulness, off-line recall measures meet with interpretative difficulties when used as indicators of the reading process. The readers' processing activities during encoding can only be inferred indirectly on the basis of data collected after encoding. Consequently, on-line measures of the actual reading process provide a recommendable complementary method. Two types of on-line methods have usually been applied: reading time measures and eye movement recordings.

(Vauras *et al.* 1992)

Skim-read questions

— what is your first reaction to the text?
— where do you think the text has come from?
— what is the text about?
— to what extent does the text arouse your interest?
— do you expect to enjoy reading the text?
— can you say why?
— how would you rate the text in terms of ease of reading or difficulty?
— can you say why?
— how easy do you think it will be to learn something from it?
— how will you have to read the text if you want to understand it and learn from it?
— what strategies will you use to understand it and learn from it?

'Comprehension' questions

—what is the 'usual' method of measuring comprehension?
—according to the authors, what is one of the major problems with retrieval rate measures of comprehension?
—what do the authors think is involved in the earlier stages of text processing?
—how is 'macrolevel coherence' defined?
—what is meant by 'microlevel coherence'?
—what do you understand by 'cohesion'?
—how would you define a 'narrative' text?
—how would you define an 'expository' text?
—give two examples of on-line research methods.
—give two examples of off-line research methods.
—do you think you can use either method in the classroom? Why?

LIMITATIONS OF STANDARD COMPREHENSION EXERCISES

From your experience of undertaking the exercise above, you have probably discovered that:
—your summary of the text was not necessarily closely related to your answers to the questions. In some exercises, comprehension, or multiple-choice questions, can be answered without reference to the text;
—conversely many questions can be answered correctly by finding just one or two words in the text;
—being able to answer the questions is not a direct reflection of how much of the text was fully understood;
—comprehension exercises do not reflect the process or outcomes of either personal or study reading;
—the texts selected for exercises are not representative of text selected for real-world personal or study reading;
—the task of answering predetermined questions is artificial, compared with real-world reflection on/discussion of what is read, or of the note-making and summarizing that is undertaken for real-world study.

It is for such reasons (and others) that the validity of the traditional comprehension or multiple-choice test has been seriously questioned in recent years.

An alternative to the comprehension test: recall measures

What then are the alternatives? For Bernhardt (1991), working within the context of foreign language reading, but drawing upon a well-established tradition in cognitive psychology and L1 reading research, the answer is recall measures, and particularly immediate recall. For teachers who wish to evaluate the potential of recall measures, Bernhardt provides an outline of procedures and guidelines for the analysis of protocols.

Standardized performance measures that have potential for diagnosis: tests developed by the assessment of performance unit

Another alternative to the more traditional comprehension test is the type of test developed by The Assessment of Performance Unit (Gorman *et al.* 1981, 1982). As was noted above, one important function of performance measures of reading is to monitor 'standards' and variation in standards, over factors like time, social class, teaching methods etc, in the reading performance of large populations of both younger and adult readers at national and, less frequently, at international levels.

In Britain and in many other countries this monitoring task is undertaken by a government-funded body; in England this body, under the umbrella of the National Foundation for Educational Research (NFER), is the Assessment of Performance Unit (APU). Over the last sixteen years, the APU has, as part of its brief, been committed to developing the tests of reading that are used in major national surveys, and that, it should be noted, must be distinguished from the tests used by many local authorities and/or other bodies, (including at times the government).

Perhaps surprisingly, it is the APU that has pioneered the development of performance tests that seek to go well beyond the limitations of other standardized measures and can be used as the basis for drawing up profiles of individual readers for diagnostic purposes. Although designed for native speakers and ESL students, the tests incorporate principles which are applicable in all reading/ learning contexts.

COMPREHENSION TESTS THAT REFLECT REAL-WORLD READING

First, in explicit recognition of the limitations of many previous performance measures, for example, sentence completion exercises, the APU team has sought to develop tests that reflect the dynamic interactive nature of real-life reading, the range of different types of texts read in real life and that involve the kinds of reading tasks required for learning purposes.

CRITERIA FOR THE SELECTION OF TEXTS

Thus the texts selected for the tests across both primary and secondary levels were 'authentic' in that they were tests that students would typically be required to read within and across the curriculum and were also likely to encounter outside school. In order to maximize the authenticity of the tasks, texts are presented in the form of thematically based booklets designed for continuity and coherence.

Overall, the texts selected fall into three broad categories: works of reference, works of literature and reading materials 'similar to those . . . read for practical purposes in daily life'. The booklets containing works of reference not only include thematically related extracts but also, as appropriate, a page of contents, an index, headings and visuals such as illustrations, charts, tables and maps. The booklets presenting works of literature are typically complete in themselves, for example, a short story or poem, or alternatively, they are made up of extracts from different sources relating to a common theme.

The everyday reading materials include extracts from such wide-ranging sources as magazines (including, for example, *Which* consumer magazine), newspapers, advertisements, forms (to be filled in), sets of instructions, notices, signs, labels and listings. For example, one booklet is in the form of a travel 'package' and contains a range of information about the resort itself, hotel accommodation, transport, entertainment, a map and a booking form.

EXERCISES THAT REFLECT REAL-WORLD READING TASKS

Unlike the traditional comprehension test, the APU tasks include open-ended questions which in many cases elicit extended answers, and/or critical response to the text, the location of information in a text, the completion of a form, the completion or construction of tables, flow diagrams and charts, labelling diagrams, and going beyond the text, for example, by writing a letter.

From this brief summary we can see that the APU tests overcome most of the criticisms of both standardized and classroom-based comprehension tests identified above. More importantly they provide a model, not only for the selection of texts for measuring and promoting comprehension, but of the kinds of reading tasks that can be used in the classroom for both testing and teaching purposes. In addition, we can see that such tests have considerable potential as the basis for drawing up profiles of individual readers. We have already seen how informal talk about texts and reading can provide a starting point for gaining an understanding of individual readers. Multi-text and multi-task measures of the kind developed by the APU provide an additional measure, one which gives us more information about what readers can actually do in different reading contexts.

PROJECT

This task is intended to help you explore your immediate professional environment in order to find out what kinds of tests of
reading performance, and what kinds of reading tasks, are used for
teaching in your own school or college and in any others to which
you have access.

One way of approaching this would be simply to informally
interview colleagues; if you do this, you should use it as an
opportunity to find out more about how your colleagues feel about
the tests and tasks they use or are required to use. Alternatively,
particularly if you are teaching in an EFL or EAP (English for
Academic Purposes) context, and are required to follow a course
book, you will find it interesting to analyse the comprehension
tasks and texts that are presented.

A further possibility, particularly for teachers following a Diploma or Masters course, would be to construct a questionnaire
that will help you collect data from a wider range of informants,
possibly following up with interviews.

Whichever task you select, it will be important to ensure that
you collect information about:
— the type of text(s) selected and why;
— the presentation of the test;
— the type of task(s) set, and in the case of questions, the type of
  questions set.

You may also wish to support your investigation by finding out
more about the APU tests, about the additional tests they have
developed for investigating students' attitudes to reading, and
about the findings of the surveys. This I would strongly recommend, particularly in view of the very limited amount of space I
have been able to give to the work of the APU.

The cloze procedure as a measure of the outcome of silent reading

We turn now to one further and also relatively familiar measure of reading performance, the use of what is known as the **cloze procedure**. The history of the cloze procedure is an interesting and complex one. Originally developed by an American journalist called William Taylor (1953), it consisted then, and now (in its pure form), of the deletion of every nth word, for example, every fifth word, as a means of measuring the relative readability of a text, that is, the match (in language and in knowledge) between a reader and the writer of a text.

The purpose of making regular deletions was, in Taylor's view, a means of achieving a random sampling of the text as a whole; the rationale here being that because there is semantic, syntactic and lexical variation within any single text, regular deletion will tap the way such variation is working across the text as a whole, and increasingly so, the longer the text. Thus, with extensive selections from rather sophisticated texts and large samples of readers, Taylor was able to demonstrate that the match between the writer of text A, and a group of readers, was greater than that between the writer of text B and the same group of readers.

The cloze procedure as a model of the reading process

In addition, the 'model' of communication on which Taylor based his 'tool for measuring readability' was in many ways a precursor of current models of the reading process. In sum the theory proposed that communication involves the 'transmission' of a message through some physical medium, for example, a telephone cable, or in the case of reading, print, and the reconstruction of this message by a 'receiver'. Taylor's specific hypothesis was that the success of the transmission would be determined by the extent of the match between the transmitter, or writer, and the receiver, or reader. And the test of this was to 'mutilate' the message in some way in order to force the receiver to reconstruct the message.

Since its development by Taylor, the use of cloze has proliferated, particularly as a procedure for developing higher-order reading skills, as a measure of comprehension, and as a diagnostic tool that provides insights into reader processes, rather than as a measure of the relative readability of different texts.

Modified cloze tasks

Increasingly, however, in both classroom (Lunzer *et al.* 1984, Davies and Greene 1984) and research contexts (Bensoussan 1990), it is modified forms of cloze that are seen to have a wide range of applications. Modified forms of cloze do not involve the deletion of every nth word, but the selective deletion of words or phrases in order to create a text-based problem-solving exercise.

MODIFIED CLOZE FOR DEVELOPING HIGHER-ORDER READING
SKILLS AND FOR DIAGNOSTIC PURPOSES

As we shall see below and in chapter 4, teachers in both L1 and L2 recognize the potential of modified forms of cloze, or word/phrase completion tasks, as a means of encouraging students to become sensitive to contextual clues in reading and as the basis for discussion of texts. In addition, when readers' responses to modified cloze tasks are recorded, they can be analysed for diagnostic purposes.

ACTIVITY

An example of a modified cloze text is presented on page 34. You are asked to study the text and then follow the steps below:
1. Find a colleague or friend who will work on the task with you.
2. Arrange to have your session taped and start recording as soon as you start the task.

3. Work with your partner to try and fill the gaps with words that fit the overall meaning and specific wording of the poem.
4. In doing this, you and your partner should try to 'justify' why you think one word is a better fit than others.

1d

MY GRANDMOTHER

She keeps an antique shop – or it kept her
Among Apostle spoons and Bristol glass,
The . . . silks, the heavy . . .
She watched her own reflection in the . . .
Salvers and . . . bowls, as if to prove
Polish was all, there was no need of . . .

And I remembered how I once refused
To go out with her, since I was afraid.
It was perhaps a wish not to be used
Like antique objects. Though she never said
That she was hurt, I still could feel the guilt
Of that refusal, guessing how she felt.

Later, too . . . to keep a shop, she put
All her best things on one long . . . room.
The place smelt . . . of things too long kept shut,
The . . . of absences where . . . come
That can't be polished. There was nothing then
To give her own . . . back again.

And when she died, I felt no grief at all,
Only the guilt of what I once refused,
I walked into her room among the tall
Sideboards and cupboards-things she never used
But needed; and no finger-marks were there,
Only the new dust falling through the air.

(Elizabeth Jennings)

When you have completed the task, you will naturally want to know what the original words were. But before you turn to these, on page 55, be reassured; the highest 'score' for this exercise when completed by either native or non-native adults speakers of English is four of the original words, and most readers are delighted if they manage to produce one word the same as the original. There are, of course, good reasons why this should be so, not least the fact that the poem is a unique meaning construct. At the same time, when you compare your own 'wordings' with those of the original you can see that most of them are in the same broad area of meaning as the original words. But the poet has the edge, and in the particular choices she makes, she reveals the subtlety of her craft.

MODIFIED CLOZE AS A WINDOW ON THE READING PROCESS

The point of the exercise then, is not to see how high, or low, scores are achieved but to gain insights into the process of reading and to see how readers go about trying to reconstruct the text. We are interested in particular in the different sources of knowledge readers draw upon in working towards an understanding of the poem, and it is the very challenge of this particular cloze task, and the range of sources of information potentially available in the task, that allow us to study readers' use of these different sources of information.

This you can do by listening carefully to the tape of your session. In doing so, try to identify evidence of your use of the following sources of information:
—syntactic knowledge, for example, knowledge about word class, such as nouns and verbs;
—knowledge about the rhyming pattern of the poem;
—knowledge about the rhythm or 'scan' of the poem, which may have influenced decisions about the length or number of syllables in a word;
—knowledge of collocation, that is, the tendency of certain words to 'go together' as in 'old and frail';

— knowledge of alliteration;

— knowledge of the real-world context of the poem, that is, of a woman who cared more for antiques than for human relationships, and knowledge of antiques.

When you listen to the tape, it is unlikely that you will find evidence of the use of all of these sources of information, but as with the use of miscue analysis, you should find evidence of the use of several sources.

In addition, you should be able to see the potential of cloze as a tool for gaining insights into the process of reading. It does this by slowing the reading process down, so that ideas about the meaning (and wording) of a text can be articulated, just as 'slow motion' images allow us to see more of what is going on in fast-moving physical actions. In this slow-motion picture of reading we also see the way readers put forward 'guesses' or hypotheses about the best fit, and then go back to the text, and/or to a collaborating partner, to confirm or revise their hypotheses. In this way, cloze provides an indirect but compelling illustration of the **interactive models of reading**, which we will study in chapter 2.

I am sure that you can also see the potential of modified cloze, with discussion, as an example of a reading activity that provides the kind of 'fun' our younger readers would like to experience in school. This is a point that will be taken up in chapter 4 when we examine the original classroom context in which the cloze task above was first used.

Cloze as a standardized measure of comprehension

Like the use of comprehension and multiple-choice questions, the cloze procedure has become the basis for a number of standardized tests of comprehension, the best-known of which are the GAP (McLeod 1970) and the GAPADOL (McLeod and Anderson 1973) tests. Like other standardized tests these serve their limited, but necessary, purposes as survey instruments, although it should be clear that they do not have the strengths of APU type measures.

CLOZE AS A MEASURE OF COMPREHENSION IN RESEARCH STUDIES

In recent years the use of a cloze test as a measure of comprehension in empirical research studies, particularly in second language reading research, has received considerable attention (Alderson 1979a and b, 1980, Alderson and Urquhart 1984, Bensoussan 1990, Jonz 1990). However, it is also the subject of considerable controversy (Bernhardt 1991), which space does not allow us to pursue here.

Cloze as the basis for research on the reading process

In the modified cloze task you have just completed, you were encouraged to record the discussion between yourself and a friend or colleague as you worked through the task. If you did this you will be aware that the recording provided data that revealed something about what you and your partner were thinking about as you sought to find appropriate completions. The data thus provided evidence of some of your internal, or introspective, thought processes.

1.2.3 Introspective methods for studying the reading process

In recent years the use of **introspective data and methods** for investigating the way in which readers process texts has become increasingly widespread in both classroom and research contexts. In such introspective studies readers are asked to report on their thought processes either as they work through a task, providing **think-aloud** data, or after they have completed a task, providing **retrospective** data. The data, or reader **protocols**, as they are known, are then analysed, typically with reference to the sources of information readers report using and/or to the strategies they report using, or can be observed using.

The protocols you recorded during the cloze task above are clearly similar to think-aloud protocols; they were collected during the task, not after it. However, because they involved a discussion, rather than a solitary individual report, I shall call them **talk-aloud**, as opposed to think-aloud data, since they are based upon what you and your partner said as you completed the task. To date, the majority of studies involving think-aloud procedures require a single subject to talk about their thinking processes while in the process of undertaking a task. However, when more than one subject is involved, the situation is slightly different, and certainly more natural; the term talk-aloud seems to me to reflect this difference.

We will see that there is a place for all three types of data collection, think-aloud, retrospection and talk-aloud. In the classroom, it seems at least initially, the participation of more than one subject and the collection of talk-aloud data has a number of advantages over single-subject studies. First, it would seem to create a more natural context for the collection of data and secondly, the interaction with another reader in itself would appear to facilitate not only the articulation of hypotheses, but also the need to justify and/or revise them. In addition, it is less likely to generate responses for the 'sake of the researcher'. It would thus appear to reflect the actual thinking going on, rather than a single subject's idea about what the researcher is interested in.

Like observational studies, introspective studies are of particular interest because they build upon the more informal methods for finding out about student reading described above. More importantly, introspective methods, like the observation and analysis of miscues, are increasingly adopted or adapted by teachers for studying the reading behaviour of their own students. In addition, as we shall see, many of the methods are not only fun for students and teachers, but also help to encourage and develop a classroom dialogue about reading, of the kind recommended above.

The use of introspective methods in both classroom and research contexts provides one way of addressing very basic questions about learning which are of interest to teachers in all contexts of education.

The potential of introspective studies

Introspective methods are thus seen to have considerable potential for providing insights, rather than firm generalizations, into the knowledge sources and strategies readers use in different reading tasks.

ACTIVITY

Consider the very general questions below, and try to decide whether you already have some of your own ideas about the answers; if you do, try to work out how those ideas were developed, for instance from a course you have attended, from reading, from the observation of your own students, or from your own experience.

—what is the range of different strategies that different readers use?
—are some sources of information and some strategies used more frequently than others?
—are some sources of information more useful in comprehension tasks than others, and if so, can they be taught?
—are some strategies more useful than others in contributing to successful performance, and if so can they be taught?
—do readers use different strategies when reading in L2 than in their native language?
—does the nature of the text, or the particular reading task make any difference to strategy use?

It is with broad questions such as those above that introspective studies are concerned and which, in recent years, have generated a body of (mostly classroom-based) research which is far too extensive to summarize here. Instead, in what follows, I shall briefly describe a limited number of studies that illustrate different introspective methods and/or analytic systems replicable in the classroom.

Examples of introspective studies

RETROSPECTION AFTER A MODIFIED CLOZE TASK

A study undertaken by Kletzien (1991) focused on sources of information and involved the collection of introspective data from 16-year-old students working on a modified cloze task and then completing a questionnaire retrospectively. Kletzien asked the questions:

— are there differences in the number and type of strategies used by 'good' and 'poor' readers?
— does the level of text make a difference to the use of strategies?

Modified cloze was chosen 'to increase students' awareness of the comprehension strategies they were using' and 'to make them aware of the thought processes they had to use to understand the passage'. Kletzien deleted content words only in order to force subjects to search beyond the immediate context. The texts were authentic and represented three levels of difficulty: independent, instructional and frustration.

As soon as the cloze tasks were completed, students were asked to go back to each word provided for the deletions and explain their thinking processes as they chose their answers. These were tape-recorded and subsequently analysed. Kletzien's method, therefore, is retrospective, that is, collecting information about the thinking process after the task.

The categories that Kletzien used for the analysis of the completions are presented on pages 42–3. We can see from this that they are mainly categories of information sources used, with only one or two strategies representing the readers' attempts to monitor or control the reading process. The results of Kletzien's study provide evidence of a range of information sources, confirming the wide variation across individuals reported at the beginning of this chapter.

The study revealed no significant differences in the number and type of strategies used by good and poor readers, except on the most difficult text (frustration level), for which the poor readers reported far fewer strategies. The strategies used by all readers varied according to the different levels of text. With the least difficult text (independent level), a much wider range of strategies was recorded and subjects also made greater use of the text as a whole. By contrast, with the frustration-level text, there was a much heavier reliance on vocabulary. In summary: 'Subjects used a broad context to construct an understanding at the independent level, focused more on the text at the instructional level and concentrated on a narrow two-or-three word base at the frustration level.'

COMBINATION OF THINK-ALOUD AND RETROSPECTIVE METHODS

For teachers who are particularly interested in the use of textual sources of information, a study by Haarstrup (1987) provides an even more detailed analysis of such sources. The study aimed to evaluate introspective methodology and contains a detailed analysis of the strengths and weaknesses of think-aloud and retrospective methods. The basic task referred to is an inferencing task, that is, one requiring students to work out the meanings of unknown words. Since this task has some features in common with cloze procedure, the categories are potentially useful.

TALK-ALOUD DATA

A study undertaken by Davies and Greene (1982), distinguishes between the use of information sources and control strategies. A small group of L1 lower secondary subjects worked on a text with the objective of completing a summary table, one of the '**active**'

CLASSIFICATION SCHEME FOR STRATEGIES

Strategy	Criteria	Sample student responses
Using syntax or punctuation	The subject's response mentions aspects of grammar, parts of speech, or punctuation.	'I put *taking* because I knew it had to be a verb.' 'I figured they were asking for another country in the list because there was a comma there.'
Using the author's style	The subject chose words to fit with the author's style.	'I was going to put shape down, but I had already used that and it didn't sound right to use it twice so I found another word for shape – *structure*.'
Using known phrases	The subject's response mentions use of a known phrase.	'*Conditions* just went with *sanitary*, that's a phrase you hear all the time.'
Rereading previous text	The subject mentions specifically going back and reading something again, or indicates using information that was more than a sentence away from the cloze blank.	'I put *Africans* because it was talking about Africans up here before. I went back and read it again.'
Reading subsequent text	The subject indicates specifically reading ahead or mentions information which is located in the sentence after one where the cloze blank appears.	'I put *geography* because the rest of this goes on to tell all about the geography. I read the rest of it before I put it in.'
Recognizing the structure of passage or paragraph	The subject's response shows that he or she recognized the author's organization of the passage or paragraph.	'They are supporting that first sentence here. They tell about something and then they are giving a reason for it. That's how they are supporting it.' 'This paragraph is giving causes. It is listing all the causes.'
Recognizing the structure of the sentence	The subject's response shows that he or she recognized the author's organization of the sentence under consideration.	'I put *reason* here because I read the rest of that sentence and they are giving a reason.'

Using prior knowledge	The subject indicates that he or she already knew something or had already experienced something (sometimes phrased as a statement of fact that the subject assumed was common knowledge).	'I put believe there because the Church does not believe in birth control. I know that for real.' 'Mountains are always covered with ice and snow.'
Visualizing	The response indicates that the subject had a picture or a mental image.	'I wasn't sure what to put here, but I put rocks because that is the image I get – rapids and rocks.'
Using the main idea	The response is based on major points of the paragraph or passage.	'This whole thing was talking about how Africa was trying to get independence so they have to have control of the government.'
Making an inference or drawing conclusions	The response indicates that the subject had made a guess or inference based on his or her own knowledge and information from the text.	'I wasn't familiar with either of these names so I simply used the fact that Charles Arden-Clarke was not an African, and Nkrumah, who was the Gold Coast Prime Minister, he was getting advice so I would assume that Clarke was an advisor. I knew he wasn't an African because of his name.'
Paraphrasing	The reason given for a cloze response includes substituting the subject's own words for the original wording of the text.	'I put *imbalance* there because it said that the high birth rate and the high death rate cancel each other out.' (The original text said, 'Latin America has a high birth rate and a high death rate which offset each other.')
Looking for key vocabulary or phrases	The response involves reasoning around a particular word or phrase. Alternatively, the subject indicates inability to fill the cloze blank because of a lack of understanding of particular words the subject views as crucial.	'I don't know if friend was right or not, but it said *sympathetic* so that is what I thought of.' 'I couldn't do that one because I don't know what *hegemony* means. I can't understand that sentence without knowing that word.'
No awareness of strategies	Response, but unable to give strategy used.	'I don't know. It just seemed to fit.'
Non-use of strategies	No response, no attempt to give strategy.	I had no idea what that one was. I couldn't even try.'

reading tasks known as **DARTs** (Directed Activities Related to Text). The researchers were concerned with the process involved in active as opposed to **passive reading tasks**. Thus, unlike most other studies reported here, the focus was not on differences in the performance of individuals or groups but on a task variable: a DARTs activity as opposed to the silent individual reading on which comprehension exercises are based. (See chapter 4 for details of DARTs.)

The specific aim of this study was to find evidence, in talk-aloud data, of the operations governing the unconscious process of reading, specifically **hypothesis generation and testing**, according to Rumelhart's (1977) interactive model of reading (see chapter 2). Davies and Greene predicted that in a DARTs task, involving talk, these unconscious processes would become overt and conscious.

To analyse the talk-aloud data, the researchers set up three categories:

1. Hypothesis generation and testing.
2. Sources of information referred to.
3. Interaction with text/other readers.

The text chosen for the activity was a description of the physical structure of a tooth.

A tooth has three regions: the crown is the part projecting above the gum, the neck is embedded in the soft gum and the root is out of sight anchoring the tooth in its bony socket. Inside the tooth is a fairly hard material which contains some living cells; this is the dentine. The dentine cannot withstand wear, so in the crown and neck it is covered with a layer of hard, non-living enamel. The dentine in the root is covered with a substance called cement, which helps to fix the tooth in its socket. Inside the dentine, in the centre of the tooth, is a hollow pulp cavity containing nerves, a small artery and a small vein. From E. J. Ewington and O. F. Moore, *Human Biology and Hygiene*.

The pupils' discussion was tape-recorded as they worked through their task of completing the summary table. A sample of the analysis of the transcript is shown on page 45.

Studying reading behaviour

ANALYSIS OF DISCUSSION TRANSCRIPT – THE TOOTH

Transcript	Student question	Student hypothesis	Hypothesis tested	Hypothesis rejected	Agreement	Text check	Text omission	Procedure check	Property of part	Location of part	Function of part
P1. Does it tell you what the crown does?	✓										✓
P2. --- protects it ---		✓				✓					
P1. Does it say that --	✓					✓					
P2. - yes, part protecting above the gum		✓				✓					
P1. - it doesn't say protecting does it --	✓					✓					
P2. -- Oh, no, projecting						✓					
P1. -- does it tell you what the crown does? -- doesn't actually does it						✓					✓
P3. It's the enamel that -- protects it -- look that's the enamel (pointing to diagram) around the crown -- 'cause your crown is enamel isn't it? -- that's what they're made of isn't it?	✓	✓	✓						✓		✓

The study provides evidence of the use of monitoring and control strategies and of the effective use of relevant information sources (in this case being the location, properties and function of the parts of the tooth). It is the only study reported to date that includes interaction with other readers as a strategy.

OBSERVATION AND RETROSPECTION

Studies based on observation of real-world classroom reading are few. One example is a study undertaken by Nicholson (1982, 1984, 1985). In this, junior high school pupils were observed and interviewed as they worked on reading tasks in normal classroom conditions in different areas of the curriculum.

Nicholson identifies a range of behaviours, the most pervasive of which are those of omission or ignoring difficult parts of the text (skipping) and straight copying. This picture of the predominance of apparently 'negative' strategies used by learners in real classroom contexts, as opposed to the experimental situation, is one that will be familiar to most teachers.

OBSERVATION AND THINK-ALOUD

A more encouraging profile of the reader as learner than that presented by Nicholson comes from recent studies by Cohen (1986) and Sarig (1987 and ms.), which led to a categorization of reading strategies. Sarig asked the question: 'Are reading processes in L1 and L2 related, and if so, in what way?' In addition, she questioned the current theoretical assumption that a certain combination of reading strategies is related to reading success and that lists of comprehension strategies can serve as the basis for curriculum planning and materials development.

The study involved ten senior high school subjects reading in both their native language, Hebrew, and the foreign language, English. The subjects represented three proficiency levels: low, intermediate and high. They were presented with two 'authentic argumentative' texts, one in Hebrew and the other in English. The task was clearly a demanding one, consisting of two parts: a 'propositional' analysis of each text, followed by the production of 'synthesis' of the text message.

Subjects were interviewed individually and recorded while thinking aloud. They were also observed. On the basis of the think-aloud data and observed behaviour, Sarig identified forty-four separate actions that she calls moves. These were classified into four broad functional categories: technical aid, clarification and simplification, coherence detecting and monitoring. For each student, a move was also evaluated as comprehension-promoting or comprehension-deterring.

Sarig's analysis reveals that different moves are not inherently effective or ineffective, but rather that it is the way in which one move combines with others and/or is followed up, that contributes to successful comprehension. However, she does observe that the monitoring move is essential for promoting comprehension. The study also found that 87 per cent of the moves were unique to individual readers, a particularly interesting result in view of the evidence of extensive reading variation in reading behaviour noted above.

INTROSPECTION, RETROSPECTION AND REVIEW

Further confirmation of the trends reported in the Sarig study also come from a more broadly based series of studies by Scott (1990). In one study, Scott focuses on the strategies readers use when reading academic texts and/or novels. The method used was delayed retrospection, or 'review' with subjects completing two written questionnaires about their normal approach to reading as opposed to their reactions after undertaking a particular task for study purposes. From the data provided by the questionnaires and interviews, Scott identified forty-one strategies, many of which are the same as Sarig's, though the labels are not identical. Furthermore, Scott's findings add support to Sarig's conclusion that no strategies are more effective than others and that there is no optimum order of using them.

ROLE OF AFFECTIVE FACTORS IN READING

A further study by Scott is one of the first attempts at exploring affective responses to reading and to text. Twenty-seven undergraduates and subsequently sixty EFL teachers were asked to provide written answers to the questions:
— what do you feel about the unknown word problem?
— what strategies do you use to infer their meanings?
— is grammar a help?
— is similarity with known words a help?
— did the presence of other unknown words make it harder or easier?

From the first set of results Scott found evidence of considerable individual variation but was able to identify three broad categories of feelings: negative, cautious and calm. In the second study, data collected from a more detailed questionnaire yielded the categories: lack of confidence, caution and confidence.

Evaluating introspective studies

From the above, the potential of introspective studies should be clear. However, researchers are becoming increasingly aware of the problems and limitations of introspective studies. Foremost amongst these is the fact that the effect of different texts has not been systematically investigated. As we shall see in chapter 3, this is in part a consequence of the fact that to date there is no consensus about how different texts and types of text might be described.

Two further variables appear to be ignored in most studies: the nature of the task and the role of affective factors. Although the Davies and Greene study indicates that the nature of the task is important, to date there is no classification of tasks to which teachers and researchers might make reference and only minimal attention has been paid to this variable in most studies. And while there is increasing interest in the role of affective factors (Scott 1990 and Oh 1990), the emphasis appears to be on anxiety rather than on a broader range of affective responses to tasks and texts.

A more widely recognized limitation of introspective methods relates to the artificial demands made on readers asked to report on their thought processes. Thus when we ask readers to report on their thinking, we need to remember that the requirement to report may interfere with the performance of the task; readers may not wish to or be able to articulate their thoughts fully; they cannot report unconscious behaviours and they may report what they think the teacher or researcher wants to hear. The reporting of one type of behaviour does not rule out the possibility of other behaviours.

A more fundamental problem is that there is wide variation across studies in the way in which behaviours are defined and classified. Thus in almost all of the studies introduced, the researchers present different categorizations or taxonomies of reading behaviour. Typically the overall term used to describe this behaviour is 'strategy'. However, this term is frequently used to refer to both sources of information and observable use of strategy. Hence the labels given to strategies by different researchers vary widely. In addition, across the different studies the kinds of behaviour classified as strategies, at least initially, appear to be almost unlimited.

PROBLEMS IN DEFINING STRATEGY

'Good' and 'bad' strategies

For some, like Hosenfeld and the EFL textbook writers following this tradition, the term strategy is typically used to refer to what are regarded as 'good' strategies, for example, skipping, going on reading etc. For others, however, particularly in view of conflicting results about which strategies are effective, the term is used neutrally. This is the position that has been adopted in this volume, and that appears to be supported by the evidence reported above.

Conscious or unconscious behaviour

A further point of dispute is whether the term strategy refers to behaviour that is deliberate and conscious or whether it can include behaviour more or less unconscious. For Cohen (1986) and Pritchard (1990) the term strategy is clearly restricted to conscious action. By contrast, Barnett (1989) uses the term to include both conscious and unconscious behaviour. Kletzien (1991) defines a strategy as 'a deliberate means of constructing meaning from text when comprehension is interrupted'. Her definition is particularly pertinent because it explicitly recognizes the distinction between the behaviour readers report when they are engaged in a reading task which intervenes in the reading process in some way, and natural reading, outside the experimental situation. In normal reading, we may surmise that many of the 'strategies' that readers use are unconscious. It is only when readers are put in a position where they are required to report on their thought processes that these may come, so to speak, to the surface of consciousness.

Drawing on Kletzien's definition, and on data from the studies reported above, the definition of strategy I would wish to propose here is that a strategy is a physical or mental action used consciously or unconsciously with the intention of facilitating text comprehension and/or learning.

However, even with the comprehensive definition of strategy proposed here, the wide variation in the categorizations of strategies makes it difficult for the teacher and researcher to compare studies. More critically it makes it very difficult for teachers to select a categorization system relevant to their own interests and practical for classroom observation.

A guide to the categorizations of strategies: types of strategy

For these reasons, I introduce here a broadly based categorization of the different **types of strategy** reported in the literature.

The categorization of the five different types of strategy identified is based first on a distinction between reported behaviour that is in some way physical and hence at least theoretically observable, such as marking the text, pausing, rereading etc, and behaviour that is not observable, such as using a particular source of information, for example, a rhyming pattern or the grammatical structure of a sentence or clause, or one's own background knowledge which is reported by the reader, and/or inferred by the researcher.

Within the non-observable category, a further distinction is made between reports of responding to or interacting with the text, by questioning the text, agreeing with the author, feeling frustrated or even 'rejecting' the text, and consciously monitoring one's own reading process, by reporting success or failure, setting goals and/or plans. These distinctions then give rise to five broad types of strategy, as presented below:

— **control reading process**, by engaging consciously or unconsciously, in action that is observable, for example, regressing, pausing, marking text;

— **monitor reading process**, by consciously attempting to find ways into the meaning of the text and/or by evaluating such attempts;

— **interact with text**, by questioning, expressing feelings etc on the basis of at least an interim interpretation of the text; hence interaction represents a response to the text rather than the evaluation of a route into the text;

— **utilize source of information**: textual, by paying attention to linguistic features of the text, and/or on one's own textual/linguistic knowledge as it is evoked by reading the text, for example, grammar, repetition of words, text structure etc;

— **utilize source of information**: external/background knowledge, by drawing on non-textual knowledge which may be evoked by,

	Kletzien	Haarstrup	Hosenfeld	Sarig	Scott	Davies & Greene	Pritchard	Block	Nicholson
CONTROL READING PROCESS				*					
Adjust rate of reading				✓					✓
Pause									✓
Regress/reread	✓			✓	✓		✓	✓	✓
Go forward in text	✓			✓			✓		
Refer to visual in text			✓						✓
Skip			✓	✓	✓		✓		✓
Use finger									
Sub-vocalize				✓					
Read aloud				✓					
Refer dictionary/glossary			✓	✓	✓				
Mark text				✓	✓			✓	
Copy								✓	
Write notes or summary				✓					
*Refer task									
MONITOR READING									
Formulate hypotheses	✓	✓	✓	✓	✓	✓	✓	✓	
Make predictions	✓		✓	✓	✓		✓		
Correct errors				✓	✓	✓	✓	✓	
Express goals				✓		✓	✓		
Refer to difficulties	✓						✓	✓	
Evaluate progress			✓	✓			✓		
Plan				✓	✓			✓	
Suspend judgement				✓			✓		
Refer task							✓		
*Reject text/task	✓			✓		✓	✓		

Studying reading behaviour

	Kletzien	Haarstrup	Hosenfeld	Sarig	Scott	Davies & Greene	Pritchard	Block	Nicholson	
UTILIZE SOURCE OF INFORMATION: Background knowledge										
Knowledge of other text(s)				✓			✓			
Knowledge of content/topic	✓	✓	✓				✓	✓		
Visual/mental picture	✓						✓			
Personal experience							✓			
Cultural knowledge							✓			
Knowledge of format							✓			
Other readers					✓	✓				
INTERACT WITH TEXT										
Question text	✓					✓	✓		✓	
Translate					✓					
Paraphrase	✓			✓			✓			
Express feelings	✓				✓		✓		✓	
*Reject text/task	✓			✓			✓		✓	
*'Learn' words					✓					
Speculate							✓			
UTILIZE SOURCE OF INFORMATION: Text										
Genre/source of text				✓						
Rhetorical structure	✓	✓		✓	✓		✓			
Information structure				✓		✓				
Register/style	✓						✓			
Immediate context		✓	✓	✓	✓		✓			
Sentence/clause structure	✓	✓		✓	✓					
Word class	✓	✓								

	Kletzien	Haarstrup	Hosenfeld	Sarig	Scott	Davies & Greene	Pritchard	Block	Nicholson
UTILIZE SOURCE OF INFORMATION: Text (cont.)									
Word meaning	✓	✓	✓		✓	✓		✓	
Lexico semantic refs.									
synonymy	✓			✓	✓			✓	
cohesion				✓					
Cognates		✓	✓		✓				
Collocation	✓	✓				✓			
Poetic feature						✓			
Phonology		✓							
Punctuation	✓								
Morphology		✓					✓		
Content/topic	✓			✓		✓			
Title/heading			✓	✓					
Text participants				✓					
Text goals				✓					

but is not given in the text, for example, knowledge of topic, content area, culture etc.

The categorization forms the basis for a review of a range of studies including, but extending beyond, those reported above, which is presented on pages 52–3. This you may find useful as a guide to the literature in that it indicates the different orientations of the studies. However, in studying the guide it is important to note first that the categories can potentially overlap; for instance, when a reader reports regressing, which would be coded as a control type of strategy, he or she may also explain why, for example, 'I wanted to check the rhyme', which would also be coded as utilizing a textual source of information. As we shall see in chapter 2, such overlap is inevitable, not only when readers report what they are doing/thinking in the slowed-down process of responding to an interviewer, but more so when they are reading 'normally' outside the experimental situation. Furthermore, it should be noted that both the categories and the strategy labels are broad summary labels based upon my own interpretation of different researchers' varying labels. For this reason they do not always reflect the original wording, and in many cases do not do justice to the finer, more delicate strategy labels presented in the different studies, in particular those of Scott and Sarig.

(Answers to activity on page 34: faded, furniture, brass, silver, love, frail, narrow, old, smell, shadows, reflection.)

SUMMARY

- Traditional measures of reading performance based on oral reading or on scores on comprehension tests are necessary for monitoring the progress of individuals and groups. With respect to measures of comprehension, the tests developed by the NFER provide a model of ways in which authentic texts and tasks can be incorporated into tests.
- However, traditional tests have limited potential as tools for teaching and learning and provide little information for teachers about how learners are developing their capacities as readers.
- Procedures which will enable teachers to study the development of individual readers all involve observation and interviews with readers and both informal and systematic analysis of students engaged in classroom reading tasks; widely tested procedures include the analysis of oral reading miscues, and the recording of readers talking and thinking aloud in problem-solving reading tasks.
- Observation and interviews with readers provide teachers with a

starting point for initiating a dialogue about reading; such a dialogue is seen to play a central role in raising student awareness of their capacities for monitoring their own reading.

- A number of taxonomies for analysing the strategies used by individual readers are available.
- However, there is as yet no agreed rationale for categorizing reading strategies and no conclusive evidence that certain strategies are inherently more facilitating of comprehension than others.
- The evidence does suggest, however, that teachers can encourage students to become increasingly aware and capable of monitoring their own reading behaviour.

2   Studying the reading process: models of reading

This chapter builds upon the methods and findings of chapter 1 in seeking an answer to the basic question: 'What goes on in the visual system and the brain during the process of reading?' From chapters 1 and 2 it will be clear that this is not an easy question to answer. None the less there is a long history of attempts to answer the question through the formulation of abstract models of the reading process. As we shall see, such models have been directly influential in the formulation of educational policies and hence have played a central, if sometimes 'hidden', role in shaping teaching methods. It is for this reason that teachers need to gain some understanding of different models and of their implications for teaching.

2.1   The concept of a model of the reading process

The term 'model' as used here refers to a formalized, usually visually represented theory of what goes on in the eyes and the mind when readers are comprehending (or miscomprehending) text. Thus we might characterize a model as a systematic set of guesses or predictions about a hidden process, which are then subjected to 'testing' through experimental studies.

In its most basic and simplified form, a model could represent the reading process as shown below, albeit supported by a detailed explanation of each stage in the model, and of what is going on in the mind at each stage.

1. Eyes look
2. Letters identified and 'sounded out'
3. Words recognized
4. Words allocated to grammatical class and sentence structure
5. Sentences give meaning
6. Meaning leads to thinking.

A model of this kind provides a description of the reading process we might consider to be a 'common sense' description; at first sight it seems to fit with what we observe in oral reading, though not perhaps with what goes on in our own reading. In addition, the model reflects certain approaches to the teaching of reading, such as phonic-based approaches, in which the sequence of instruction is intended to reflect the assumed sequence of processing: from letters to sounds, to words, to sentences and finally to meaning and thinking. A model that represents such a sequence is known as a **bottom-up** model of the reading process.

There are, however, alternative ways of representing the process of reading. One alternative is a model of reading in which the processing sequence is almost the reverse of that above. This is illustrated below.

1. Eyes look
2. Thinking – predictions about meaning
3. Sample sentence as a whole to check meaning
4. To check further, look at words
5. If still uncertain study letters
6. Back to meaning predictions.

By contrast with the bottom-up model, this model includes thinking and meaning at a very early stage, and the processing sequence proceeds from predictions about meaning to attention to progressively smaller units. Such a model is known as a **top-down model** and is one which may appear to capture something of the essence of our own experience of reading.

In the literature on the reading process, both bottom-up and top-down models are represented, and both have been influential in the development of policies and methods for the teaching of reading. Since each type of model presents a contrasting view of reading, the models have given rise to continued controversy about the methods used to study the reading process and the methods used to teach reading. Before we take a closer look at bottom-up and top-down and other models in the literature, you should consider the influence of either or both models on your own experience of reading and the teaching of reading.

ACTIVITY

Consider the following questions:
— what kind of evidence is used to support top-down or bottom-up models of reading?
— should models of reading influence teaching methods?
— in what ways might models of reading influence teaching methods?
— to what extent do the materials and methods used in your own classroom assume a top-down or bottom-up model of processing?
— what kind of model is applicable to the behaviour of different groups of readers, for example, beginning L1 readers, fluent adults reading in the native tongue, L2 beginners, or advanced readers?

2.2 Two contrasting models of the reading process

In the view of many researchers involved in studying the reading process, we should be very cautious about extrapolating from research to classroom practice. However, two contrasting models that have been particularly influential are those of Gough (1972), representing a bottom-up view of the reading process, and Goodman (1969, 1970, 1975 and 1988), representing a top-down picture of the process.

2.2.1 A bottom-up model as support for phonic-based methods of teaching reading

The evidence on which Gough based his model was drawn from laboratory studies of adult readers engaged in letter and word recognition tasks. On the basis of these studies, Gough characterizes reading as a letter-by-letter progression through text, with letter identification followed by the identification of the sounds of the letters until words, their syntactic features and then meanings are finally accessed. From this it would seem that Gough's model characterizes reading as being rather laborious, and that it implies that the teaching of reading should reflect the sequential processing of a bottom-up model of reading. For this reason, models like Gough's are used to support phonic approaches to the teaching of reading which focus attention on letter-to-sound correspondence at the expense of other sources of information. In addition, Gough challenges top-down models which emphasize the importance of predicting, or guessing, in learning to read. However, as we shall see below, evidence from more recent research does not support Gough's view of the reading process.

The complexity of grapho-phonic rules

One of the weaknesses of the model as a basis for teaching, as Smith (1971) demonstrates, is that it does not account for the fact that there are at least 166 different **grapho-phonic rules** covering the regular spelling-to-sound correspondences of English words and that these are 'not easy to teach'. Furthermore, the serial processing proposed by Gough imposes a very heavy burden on short-term or working memory. In beginning reading such a burden can be counter-productive, forcing the reader to focus on lower-level sources of information such as letter–sound correspondences at the expense of other sources of information.

2.2.2 A psycholinguistic model emphasizing top-down processing

By contrast with Gough's bottom-up model, the top-down models that have been developed within the theoretical framework of psycholinguistics, particularly those of Smith (1971, 1973) and Goodman (1969, 1970, 1975 and 1985), pay minimal attention to letter–sound correspondences, and place their emphasis on 'higher-order' sources of information. Of the two relatively compatible sources of theory, it is Goodman's 'unlimited macro' model which we will examine, since it is the most frequently cited in both L1 and L2 literature.

Unlike Gough's model which was based on studies of fluent adult readers, Goodman's model was based on the study of beginning L1 readers. However, just as Gough extrapolates from studies of adult readers to beginners, so Goodman extrapolates from beginning readers to fluent adults.

Reading as a psycholinguistic 'guessing game'

The distinctive feature of this psycholinguistic model is Goodman's emphasis on the central directing role of reader predictions with minimum attention to visual decoding. Thus 'prediction precedes confirmation which precedes correction'. The reading process is represented as a series of four primary cycles: optical, perceptual, syntactic and meaning, with meaning in the controlling role: 'the readers' focus, if they are to be productive, is on meaning, so each cycle melts into the next and the readers leap towards meaning.'

In this model, anticipation and prediction are the driving forces and the task of processing visual information is reduced merely to the recognition 'of a graphic display as written language', which 'normally occurs only once in each reading activity'. From this it is clear that Goodman's leaper towards meaning presents a sharp contrast to Gough's (1972) plodder through print.

Implications for teaching: the role of prediction

In further contrast to Gough's model, Goodman's model is explicitly aimed at effecting radical changes in teaching methodology, and has been widely influential in both L1 and L2, particularly in promoting the importance of prediction, guessing and 'going for gist' at the expense of attention to letters and words. However, just as recent evidence has cast serious doubts on Gough's bottom-up model, so too has it revealed weaknesses in Goodman's leaping to meaning model. In addition, in its very strong emphasis on prediction at the expense of attention to detail, the model has exposed itself to complete rejection in certain educational contexts, with the result that the strengths of the model are ignored in favour of more simplistic bottom-up models such as that of Gough.

But perhaps the most serious criticism of the model is that it claims, on the basis of data from L1 beginners, to represent the behaviour of efficient fluent readers. Equally worrying, as Bernhardt (1991) observes, is the widespread application of the model to L2 reading. Eskey (1988) too, observes that the application of top-down models to L2 learning 'has resulted in many useful insights, but lack of attention to decoding problems has, I think, produced a somewhat distorted picture of the true range of problems second language readers face.'

Against this background, however, there is clear evidence that the Goodman model may, indeed, offer a reasonably 'truthful' representation, though not an explanation, of the behaviour of beginning L1 readers. More importantly there is clear evidence that the methodology of miscue analysis on which the model was based is not only theoretically robust, but is also of direct and continuing practical application.

2.3 An alternative to bottom-up and top-down models: Rumelhart's interactive model

From the above, it should be clear that there are serious problems inherent in both strictly bottom-up or top-down models. We turn now from our consideration of recognized bottom-up and top-down models to a model that seeks to account for both bottom-up and top-down processing: the interactive model proposed by Rumelhart (1977). Since this model is currently the most influential model underpinning both L1 and L2 approaches to reading, the model and various developments and applications of the model are presented in detail.

Rumelhart's (1977) model (and subsequent updates of the model, Rumelhart (1984) and McClelland *et al.* (1986), represents the first of a number of interactive models of reading. Rumelhart's objective was to propose an alternative to serial, bottom-up models by incorporating the possibility of **parallel processing**, that is the simultaneous processing of information from more than one source.

The model developed from laboratory research on fluent skilled readers, which demonstrates the interaction between different sources of information. They include examples of the identification of a letter being determined by the word in which it appears, of the identification of a word being dependent upon the semantic and syntactic context in which it appears, and the interpretation of a text being dependent upon the schematic framework within which it is presented. The model is presented on page 64.

2.3.1 Selective use of different information sources

Unlike bottom-up and top-down models, the interactive model does not predict any predetermined direction for, or sequence of,

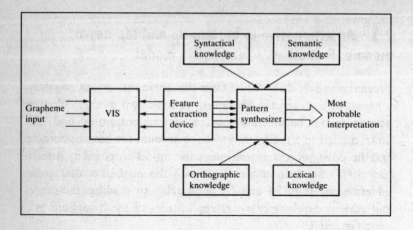

processing. Instead, the reader is seen to be able to draw simultaneously, but selectively, upon a range of sources of information:
visual, orthographic, lexical, semantic, syntactic and schematic.

In contrast to top-down models, however, the model does pay
considerable attention to visual information, and like bottom-up
models, incorporates a feature analytic mechanism for the processing of visual information. For Rumelhart, the process of reading

begins with a flutter of patterns on the retina and ends (when successful)
with a definite idea about the author's intended message. Thus reading is
at once a 'perceptual' and 'cognitive' process. Moreover, a skilled reader
must be able to make use of sensory, semantic and pragmatic information
to accomplish his task. These various sources of information appear to
interact in many complex ways during the process of reading. (Rumelhart
1977, pages 573–4)

The model itself is transparent from the diagram. The process
starts with graphemic information being registered in a Visual
Information Store (VIS). Here the graphemic input is operated on
by a feature extraction device. These features are then fed into the
pattern synthesizer, which has access simultaneously to information
about orthography, syntax, lexis and semantics. Thus 'all sources

of knowledge come together at one place and the reading process is the product of the simultaneous joint application of all knowledge sources.'

What the model does not show is how these sources interact. In explanation, Rumelhart proposes a set of parallel interacting processes which are controlled by a message centre. This keeps a set of running hypotheses about the nature of the input string which are either confirmed or disconfirmed; the search is basically for 'the right fit'. The role of the message centre is of particular interest since it is responsible for the monitoring strategies that were referred to in chapter 1 in the study by Sarig. This would indicate that it deserves much more attention in the teaching of reading.

2.3.2   A model that accounts for different kinds of reading behaviour

The most obvious strength of the model is that it provides an alternative to both bottom-up and top-down models. In addition, it offers an explanation of why Goodman's young readers do rely so heavily on semantically driven guessing, since they are still learning to process letters and words automatically, and why fluent adult readers do not, since they do not (mostly) need to guess the identity of words.

In addition, the model makes it possible to hypothesize that when readers are inexperienced at processing visual and orthographic information they will rely more heavily on semantic information, as Stanovich (1980) has demonstrated. When syntactic knowledge is poor, a greater reliance may be placed on orthographic or lexical information. And it is possible to test these predictions. Thus the model provides a basis for investigations of the performance, and indeed the processing strategies of different groups of readers under different conditions, L1 or L2.

2.3.3 A model for both L1 and L2

The potential of an interactive model for second language pedagogy is recognized by Eskey, who observes: 'It can, for example, accommodate the problems of developing less than fluent readers such as second language readers, who seem to need as much help in "holding in the bottom" (that is in simple decoding) as they do in performing higher-level interpretations of texts.'

Furthermore, an interactive model lends support to the importance in beginning L1 reading of encouraging learners to become sensitive to all sources of information rather then relying on one source, for example, letter–sound correspondences, as Gough would recommend, or on another, such as prior expectations, as Goodman would have it. Thus this model adds weight to the role, in beginning reading, of miscue analysis and of mixed methods of teaching.

2.3.4 A development of the interactive model: schema theory

In more recent studies, Rumelhart (1984) has amplified the 1977 model by paying greater attention to the role of the semantic level of processing, proposing a 'schema-theoretic' account of the comprehension process. As we shall see, the focus here is on higher levels of processing rather than on lower-level processing of visual information, although it should be noted that lower-level processing is not ignored. In this explanation the basic construct proposed is a **schema**, defined as a unit of knowledge. The function of schemata is to provide frameworks for interpreting the world, including, in reading, the world of the text. The fundamental assumption is that we can only interpret visual information and words by relating these to our prior knowledge and experience; and our prior knowledge and experience is seen to be 'packaged' into an infinite number of both general and specific units or schemata. Furthermore, an individual's schemata may change over time and with experience. From this it should be clear that schemata should not be thought of as fixed and stable but rather as fluid and constantly subject to modification.

Rumelhart's methodology: on-line processing

To test his theory of a schema-driven comprehension process, Rumelhart developed a methodology that involved on-line processing techniques. These techniques can be applied in the classroom to encourage awareness of the reading process and are further examples of activities that are fun (see chapter 4).

In one technique readers are presented with a text or 'story' in stages and asked the basic question: 'What is going on here?' This generates a prediction, which is subsequently confirmed or rejected by further exposure to the text. The technique was designed to demonstrate that in the comprehension process readers draw upon their schemata and then check their schematic 'predictions' as they progress through the text. Rumelhart calls these predictions **hypotheses**, and the testing of the hypotheses evaluation.

ACTIVITY

In a now classic example, subjects were presented with the text below (<u>one sentence at a time</u>) and asked at each stage to answer 'where/what/when/who/why' questions. The results showed that in response to the question about location, subjects produced different hypotheses after the first sentence. However, after reading one or more of the subsequent sentences, the majority changed their hypotheses. By the time the fourth sentence had been presented, all readers had arrived at a 'correct' interpretation.

Try the experiment with your own subjects, presenting each sentence at a time and allowing time for discussion between subjects, and then analyse the information sources used.

2a

THE OIL CRISIS

> *Business had been slow since the oil crisis.*
> *Nobody seemed to want anything really elegant any more.*
> *Suddenly the door opened and a well-dressed man entered the showroom floor.*
> *John put on his friendliest and most sincere expression and walked towards the man.*

(Rumelhart 1984)

The potential of the on-line prediction technique for helping us to understand the different sources of information which readers draw upon when undertaking a task like this is increasingly recognized by teachers in both L1 and L2 contexts.

In my own informal studies I have been able to record the discussions of groups of teachers from different backgrounds and cultures as they completed and discussed their predictions line by line. From my analysis of these discussions, it is evident that cultural background and readers' knowledge of the world, or content knowledge, appear to influence predictions and to shape initial predictions in quite powerful ways; gender too appears to play a part.

Different types of schemata?

The notion of different types of schemata has become of increasing interest to a number of researchers in recent years and is represented in a series of studies undertaken by Carrell (1983b, 1984, 1987), who seeks to distinguish between formal schemata and content schemata. However, the question of the relative stability and separateness of these two information sources remains unanswered. The evidence from the studies reported in chapter 1 is that at any stage of processing, different sources of information interact with each other and are utilized in unpredictable ways which are not open to direct observation.

This supports Rumelhart's views above that schemata are not stable and fixed as Carrell assumes, but rather constantly in a state of fluidity. This view is reinforced in Rumelhart *et al.* (1986).

2.4 A bottom-up interactive model

A model that seeks to account in detail for the utilization of all sources of information is a recent model proposed by Rayner and Pollatsek (1989), which they describe as bottom-up interactive. The label bottom-up emphasizes the importance Rayner and Pollatsek place on the processing of visual information. Like Rumelhart, Rayner and Pollatsek base their model on laboratory studies of fluent adult readers. As the basis of their model they provide a comprehensive and detailed account of the methods used to study the reading process and report more recent findings that emerge from such studies.

In contrast with Gough's strictly serial bottom-up model this more recent bottom-up model is an example of recent and current models which aim to be as bottom-up as possible but none the less incorporate 'interactive' features: 'our model is primarily bottom-up, but top-down processes do interact with bottom-up processes.'

As a bottom-up model it is most detailed in its account of visual processing and is based upon data from extensive and sophisticated studies of eye movements. The objective is to demonstrate the relationship between eye movements and cognitive processing.

The process of reading is seen to start with a fixation of the **fovea**, or focusing mechanism, of the eyes on a stretch of print. From their experimental data, Rayner and Pollatsek observe that the **eye fixation** is limited to a (universal) **perceptual span**, which extends only to about fifteen characters.

2.4.1 Automatic identification of words

This leads to the identification of about one to three words and their meanings either directly, from visual information, or indirectly through reference to grapho-phonic 'rules'. This latter option allows for the activation of inner speech. Whichever route is chosen, with fluent adult readers it typically leads to the automatic identification of words, which is calculated from experiments to be as rapid as 60–70 msecs.

2.4.2 Interaction of information sources

However, this automatic identification of words is seen to be partially influenced by the thematic processor in which lexical, syntactic, semantic and background knowledge interact. But it is the automatic recognition of words, in this model, which is seen to free up the processing time to allow for interaction with higher-level sources of information. The thematic processor appears to be the controlling mechanism and to fulfil the same function as Rumelhart's message centre.

2.4.3 Implications for teaching

The importance of visual information and words

The evidence from the model presented by Rayner and Pollatsek, I suggest, has a number of implications for teaching. The first of these is the evidence that they present that comprehension cannot proceed without attention to visual information and words. Reading occurs during fixations of the eyes (however hard this is to observe in the classroom), not when the eyes are moving, or 'skimming', over text. Furthermore, there is a limit to how much text can be seen (about fifteen characters) and processed during a fixation.

Time needed for processing

A second implication for teaching is the proposal in the model that different sources of information compete for processing time. This has particular relevance for beginning readers whose word recognition may not be automatic. The model suggests that when extra time is used for visual processing or word identification, there is less time available for attention to other sources of information, such as semantic or background knowledge. There is a need, therefore, to allow for the fact that L2 beginning readers particularly, as we shall see below, may need extra time to process visual information and words.

Individual reading styles

In proposing an optional, phonological processing route, the model also allows for the possibility that for some readers, or many readers under certain conditions, 'sounding out' may be necessary. Thus the model further confirms the picture of individual reading styles and strategies suggested by Sarig, and indicates the need for teachers to encourage readers to monitor their own reading, rather than to seek to control it by prescribing specific strategies.

Strengths of the model

Although Rayner and Pollatsek insist that they have not discovered 'the truth about reading', their model does provide a rich source for hypotheses, serving to fill in some of the aspects of reading not accounted for in either the Goodman or the Gough models, and at the same time being compatible with Rumelhart's interactive model.

At a more practical level, the model clearly provides support for the mixed methods approach to the teaching of beginning reading recommended by HMIs in their 1991 Report, and within the National Curriculum (1990); in an L2 context, it also lends support to Eskey's call for greater attention to lower-level decoding processes in L2, and for attention to monitoring processes at all levels of reading in both L1 and L2.

2.5   A model that incorporates affective factors

In view of the findings in chapter 1, it is appropriate that we include a model that incorporates affective factors in reading. The model most explicit in its predictions about affective factors is that of Mathewson (1985). This model takes account of the real-world context of reading in ways that other models do not, starting indeed at the level of deciding whether or not to read. And it is the affective factors, attitude, motivation, affect and physical feelings that serve as the input to this initial decision-making process.

2.5.1   Affective factors in reading

Thus <u>attitude</u> is seen to represent 'values, beliefs and interests', and includes readers' attitudes to the features of text such as content, format; for example, layout and visuals, and form; for example, register, style, dialect etc. It also includes more general attitudes to reading such as liking or disliking it, feeling that it is important or not, etc.

Closely related to attitude in the model, but none the less treated as a distinct variable, is <u>motivation</u>. Amongst the different motives proposed by Mathewson are those of 'belongingness, esteem, self-actualization, the desire to know and understand and aesthetic need.'

The third component, <u>affect</u>, is seen in turn to be closely related to, but distinct from, attitude and motivation and includes moods, sentiment and emotion.

Finally, with the specification of the component <u>physical feelings</u> in the model, Mathewson reminds us further of the real-world context in which reading may occur. 'Physical feelings arising from outside sources sometimes occur during reading, or physical feelings related to the meaning of the reading material itself sometimes intrude themselves into the reader's consciousness.'

2.5.2 Primary and secondary reading processes

The functioning of the model is initiated by the unweighted input from the four affective factors. If these result in the decision to read, or continue reading, then the primary reading processes are activated. These are seen as physical orientation and activity, attention and comprehension. In contrast to previous models, these primary reading processes receive minimal attention.

In further contrast to previous models, a set of secondary processes is proposed. These are recall, reflection and application and they interact with the primary processes. Consistent with his real-world orientation, Mathewson reports that 'The secondary component was added because it appeared to be important that readers do more with reading materials than merely read them.'

2.5.3   Implications for teaching

In drawing attention to the possibility that attitude and motivation are central, and indeed prior, conditions for successful reading, the model has far-reaching implications for teaching. Not least is the implication that instructional prescriptions, even if appropriate, will be unheeded in the absence of positive attitudes and motivation.

2.6   Towards an integration of models

A starting point for evaluating the different models is their similarities: all are based on the assumption that reading starts with a visual stimulus, and that when comprehension takes place, it ends with meaning. Moreover, all take it as axiomatic that readers are driven by a search after meaning, and most recognize that visual, orthographic, phonological, syntactic, semantic, discourse and real-world knowledge play a part in the process. In addition, Mathewson's model draws attention to affective factors.

It is the relative emphasis each model places on these different sources of information that principally differentiates them. This emphasis, in turn, is frequently a direct reflection of the methodology and data upon which the model is based. Thus the different models together provide teachers with a rich source of hypotheses about the utilization of different sources of information in reading. However, the question they do not answer or even ask is: 'Under what conditions, how, and to what extent, is each source of information utilized in reading in the context of learning?' It is this practically oriented question that has been addressed in a study undertaken by Hedge (1991).

2.7 A development from reading models: a taxonomy of modes and anchors

The study undertaken by Hedge does not offer a model, but as an alternative presents a taxonomy of reading behaviours called **modes**, knowledge sources utilized in reading called **anchors**, and reading purposes called **drivers**.

In contrast to the models described above, the study and the taxonomies are based on the analysis of introspective data collected from adult readers of EFL who were preparing for, or actually undertaking, postgraduate study in a British university, and as preparation or support for that study were following a course in English for Academic Purposes (EAP). In addition, as an informal 'control', Hedge collected introspective data from fluent L1 adult readers.

2.7.1 Applying a reading model to classroom-based observation of reading

One of the objectives of Hedge's study was to test the applicability of various abstract models of the reading process to the actual reading behaviour of this specific group of EAP readers. The specific problem Hedge sought to address was that while she found interactive models the most plausible as explanations of the 'idealized' behaviour of the reading process, the behaviour predicted by the model did not seem to be exhibited by the readers she was teaching.

Conversely, what her initial observations indicated was that some readers appeared to adopt bottom-up processing behaviour, others top-down strategies and even others interactive behaviour. In addition, there was evidence that the individual behaviour of both L2 and L1 readers varied during the course of reading a single text, and also in response to different texts.

Reading mode	Description of reading behaviour
Interactive	uses all available knowledge sources from text to content, genre and world knowledge
Top-down, relative data exclusion	uses predominantly conceptual [content, genre, world] knowledge to the relative or selective exclusion of text data
Top-down, deferred interactive	uses all available knowledge sources from text to concepts but processes top-down before bottom-up before synthesizing to attain an interactive network of comprehension
Bottom-up, non-recursive	uses predominantly text data to the relative exclusion of conceptual knowledge and does not reread or consider previous text
Bottom-up, recursive	uses predominantly text data to the relative exclusion of conceptual knowledge but does reread or consider previous text
Bottom-up, recursive, deferred interactive	uses all available knowledge sources from text to concepts but processes bottom-up, recursive before top-down before synthesizing to attain an interactive network of comprehension

2.7.2 From reading models to modes of reading

In order to attempt a descriptive framework of reading behaviour, Hedge undertook analyses of the introspective data collected from both individuals and groups of readers typically engaged in silent reading of authentic texts, followed by discussion of the texts and of any difficulties, or breakpoints, encountered. On the basis of these analyses she identified seven distinct modes of reading, subsequently reduced to six, shown above.

From this table it is clear that the notion of modes not only accommodates the possibility of a fully interactive and automatic mode of processing, as predicted by the models, but also of deferred

KNOWLEDGE ANCHORS:		
LINGUISTIC	LEXICO–SEMANTIC	
	LEXICAL STRUCTURAL	
	DISCOURSE	
	GENRE, TEXT–TYPE	
CONTENT	GENERAL .... SPECIFIC	

interactive processing, following the utilization of either top-down information sources, or bottom-up sources of information.

In addition, it also allows for the possibility of processing being predominantly top-down, or predominantly bottom-up. What the taxonomy does not include, it should be noted, is the utilization of the most bottom-up level of information, the actual visual input. This is an inevitable limitation of classroom-based, non-laboratory studies.

2.7.3 Knowledge sources used in reading

However, this limitation is compensated for by the taxonomy of the knowledge sources, or anchors, which Hedge proposes are potentially available in the reading task. These are summarized above. In her specification of these anchors Hedge's objective was to redirect attention to lower-level sources of information as well as to the higher-order sources which have received such emphasis in L2 studies. In addition, she makes no assumptions about the relative separability of different sources or about their stability. Indeed her observations consistently provide evidence of readers 'shifting' their attention from one knowledge source to another in the period of a few minutes of reading.

Thus, in combination, the taxonomies of modes and anchors provide a framework for analysing readers' changing behaviours as they read a text, and serve to reveal the central interaction between the next most bottom-up source of information, the words on the page, and the readers' utilization of higher-level sources of information.

2.7.4   Reader purposes as 'drivers' of the reading process

From her observations, Hedge also became increasingly aware that readers' purposes could have an influence on the mode of reading adopted and on the anchors utilized. Here studies show, for example, that in certain circumstances readers may have both comprehension and language-learning purposes.

Thus Hedge proposes a third parameter for the analysis of reading, the notion of 'drivers'. These comprise four broad purposes: meaning, gist, language acquisition and/or language acquisition/ meaning. From the terminology chosen it would appear that Hedge assumes that readers' purposes not only play an important part in the process of reading but that they perhaps control, or 'drive' it. Such a view would be consistent with the role of the message centre in Rumelhart's model and of the thematic processor in Rayner and Pollatsek's model. It would also be consistent with the evidence in chapter 1 of the importance of monitoring strategies. The evidence would again suggest that as teachers we cannot prescribe how our students should work at texts, but rather help them constantly to monitor and evaluate their own performance.

With this brief introduction, the potential of Hedge's modes, anchors and drivers as a framework for studying reading behaviour in the classroom is also indicated. In Hedge's study the readers were adult readers in EAP, but the methodology is equally applicable to both L1 and L2 students reading for purposes of learning. It is to a consideration of the potential of the models for developing reading in different contexts that we now turn.

2.8 Towards implications for teaching

2.8.1 Beginning mother tongue readers

It might be predicted that in the early stages of reading the beginning L1 reader will rely very heavily on schematic knowledge, on prior predictions, on syntax and on familiar vocabulary, as he or she will be unable to process as much visual information as adults. And this is the picture of the beginning reader which the psycholinguistic model presents. As we have seen above, however, it is not an accurate picture of what the reader will be doing as he or she gains proficiency.

Beginning readers in the mother tongue, therefore, should be solidly rooted in a context that allows the reader to exploit his or her internal resources arising from familiarity with the spoken language and culture, such as well-established schemata for narrative, rhyme and humour. Teachers should aim at helping the reader to become gradually more sensitive to the potential of the graphic display and its inevitably complex relationship with the phonological system of the language. The evidence also points strongly to the advantages of mixed methods in the teaching of beginning reading.

2.8.2 Skilled readers in L1 schooling

The group of 'skilled' readers referred to here included all students who have mastered the basic process of decoding, but who are still limited in the range of words or wordings they can process 'automatically' and in the range of texts they can comprehend and/or learn from effectively.

It is in this context that Rumelhart's schema theory of reading has most to contribute. The aims must be to help students extend their real-world and schematic knowledge, their mental and reading lexicon and the range of texts to which they are exposed, and to provide them with tools for gaining access to the purpose and structure of different texts and for helping them monitor their own reading and study strategies. Equally important, as predicted by Mathewson's model, will be the need to find ways of encouraging motivation and of recognizing the role of other affective factors.

2.8.3 EAP/ESP adult reading in a foreign language

By contrast with the beginning reader, the adult reader of a foreign language starts with certain advantages as a visual processor. The first of these is an adult perceptual span of about fifteen characters.

If they are fluent in their native language, these readers will have well-established schemata for reading a wide range of texts in the mother tongue, a rich mental lexicon and well-established strategies for monitoring and checking their own reading. However, they will lack knowledge of the phonology, syntax and vocabulary of the target language, and again to varying degrees, knowledge of the culture of the target language (though here it should be noted that there are 'cultures' such as those of specialist subjects and professions that cross language communities).

It may be predicted then that in the early stages of reading in a foreign language, adult readers may be forced, even more than beginning readers in their mother tongue, to rely heavily on background knowledge. More seriously, it may also be predicted that adult readers fluent in their mother tongue will find this very frustrating. As a consequence it seems likely that this frustration will result in the adoption of strategies to compensate in some way. For some readers such compensation may lead to a 'bottom-up' focus on visual information or isolated lexical items; for others, exposed to the skipping–guessing orthodoxy of many EFL textbooks, to a reliance on top-down prediction with minimal attention to visual information and lexical items. The possibility of either route would be predicted by Rumelhart's model, and the strong effect of affective factors is predicted by Mathewson's model.

2.8.4 L2 learners reading in secondary school

Unlike the groups of readers above, who for the most part have a basic need to read either in their mother tongue or in L1, L2 learners reading in the context of learning a foreign language start with a potential disadvantage, that is that they may have neither an intrinsic nor extrinsic need to read. In addition, they will have many of the linguistic and cultural disadvantages of the EAP or ESP adult reader, with more limited resources for overcoming them. From this it is clear that Mathewson's model should suggest implications for teaching.

The first of these is the prior importance of motivation and the need to establish real-world purposes for reading. The second is the need for the selection of texts that are not only of interest to the students but are representative of the types of texts with which students will be familiar in their first language. As with L1 readers in school, the reading programme should provide regular opportunities for students to learn how to become aware of their own reading processes and to monitor them.

In view of Rayner's and Pollatsek's account of visual processing, teachers should also be willing to tolerate and provide support for slow and laborious processing at early stages of learning and should not exhort students just to go for gist and ignore words, since the acquisition of word recognition skills and knowledge of word meaning will be fundamental to progress.

SUMMARY

- The evidence suggests that no single model of reading accounts for the complex range of reading behaviours which are observable in different contexts.
- However, each of the different models can contribute in different ways to our understanding of reading behaviour in different contexts.
- Thus a psycholinguistic model demonstrates the extent to which beginning L1 readers rely heavily on syntactic, semantic and (narrative) schematic knowledge, arising from familiarity with the spoken language and culture. However, a bottom-up interactive model strongly suggests that such knowledge is insufficient for further development and needs to be supplemented by attention to visual information, orthography and sound–symbol correspondences.
- Rumelhart's schema theory of reading contributes most to our understanding of skilled readers in an L1 context. Mathewson's model of affective factors in reading also indicates the importance of motivation and of individual response to text at this stage.
- In the context of L2 adult EAP/ESP reading, the contribution of Rayner's and Pollatsek's bottom-up interactive model of reading is to draw attention to the importance of the visual, lexical and syntactic features of a language different from the mother tongue, indicating the need for students to take time to acquire automatic processing of such features. In this process it may be

predicted that students will have a choice between relying upon well-established schematic knowledge, or processing bottom-up information incrementally, and that such a choice will be influenced by affective factors. In an EAP/ESP context a strong motivation to learn may compensate for difficulties, although some frustration for readers already fluent in their mother tongue is likely.

- All models suggest that those studying <u>English as a foreign language in school</u> will be even further disadvantaged than the groups above with less well-established schemata and knowledge of the conventions of the foreign language. In addition, the kind of motivation that will provide support for the adult learner cannot be assumed. For teachers of such students it would appear that Mathewson's model should provide a starting point, suggesting the prior importance of motivation and the need to establish real-world purposes and texts for reading.

3 Towards a practical framework for describing and analysing texts

In this chapter we turn from studying the process of reading to look more closely at the basic resources for reading, the texts which we, or our students, can select for the reading classroom, and which we can analyse as the basis for designing reading activities.

The text as a variable has received only minimal attention in investigations of the process of reading, and, as noted above, there is no agreed framework to date for describing different kinds of texts. In this book the text is given central importance and is seen to be the variable (together with task) that will most strongly influence the motivation to read, the approach to reading and the type of reading adopted.

In this chapter we examine different ways of describing texts and different approaches to the analysis of the structure, function and language of different texts. Thus part 1 of the chapter deals with definitions of text and examines ways of describing differences amongst texts. This provides the basis of a practical framework for describing different classes and constituents of text. In part 2, different procedures for analysing texts as the basis for course design are introduced.

PART 1: TEXTS, CLASSES OF TEXTS AND CONSTITUENTS OF TEXT

3.1 Towards a definition of text

One of the most influential definitions of **text** is that provided by Halliday and Hasan (1976):

A text is a unit of language in use . . . and it is not defined by its size . . . A text is best regarded as a semantic unit: a unit not of form but of meaning. A text has **texture** and that is what distinguishes it from something that is not a text. It derives this texture from the fact that it functions as a unity with respect to its environment. (Halliday and Hasan 1976, pages 1–2)

More recently, in Halliday and Hasan (1985/89), the criterion of texture is supplemented by that of **structure**: 'Texts are characterized by the unity of their structure and the unity of their texture'.

In both definitions, the centrality of individual writer purpose (a text is for the expression/communication of meaning) and of **cohesion**, which is what contributes to texture, is fundamental. In the second definition, the inclusion of the criterion of structure suggests that for a text to be text, it should somehow be complete. We will return to this notification of completeness below. At this point we can see that the definitions of text above allow us to distinguish between stretches of print that can count as texts and those that cannot, as in the examples below.

Consider:

3a
On Sunday morning, Louis hopped out of his bed at an early hour as usual and dashed into the 'big' bedroom where his parents slept. All ready to leap on to them for 'wake-ups' and games, he stopped – and looked again. There was someone strange in the bed. In fact two strange people – humped under the bedclothes and faintly snoring.

3b

The boy hopped and leapt. Two strange people humped under the bedclothes and faintly snored. Some people wake up at six o'clock. Leaping wakes people up. Louis liked the early hours. The parents slept. He looked again. He stopped. Louis dashed into the big bedroom. (Author's data)

3.1.1   Coherence of a text: a function of structure and texture

Text **3a** is clearly coherent and counts as text. It has structure in that the sentences are ordered according to a recognizable chronological sequence and with respect to the clause relations of cause and effect: *he stopped – and looked again* [why?] because *there was someone strange*. It has texture in that there are clear linguistic links between sentences: we know, for instance, that the *he* refers to Louis throughout, and that *his* refers to Louis's parents.

By contrast, with an effort, and because of the influence of text **3a**, we can make some sense out of text **3b**, but we are unlikely to judge it as **coherent**. This is because it lacks structure and texture. This lack is of course relative; in practice, we find that texts can be more or less coherent, more or less well-structured and more or less cohesive.

3.2   Ways of describing differences amongst texts

In practice, readers rarely have difficulty in making judgements about the relative coherence of a text. However, when they are asked to make judgements about differences amongst texts their criteria vary widely, indicating that there is a range of different aspects or features of text which are used to describe differences. Amongst these features are those of readability, content, affective impact, rhetorical function, rhetorical patterns and source of text.

3.2.1   Difficulty and readability

For many teachers the relative difficulty of a text is an important feature and potential sources of difficulty have been identified by Perera (1984).

The **readability** of a text has traditionally been measured through reference to formulae that take account of word and sentence length and complexity, or, as we saw in chapter 1, through the use of the cloze procedure. For both L1 and L2 teachers concerned with the relative difficulty of texts, readability, as measured formally or informally is still an important feature of a text, and details can be found in Harrison. In an EFL context there is also a concern with the relative difficulty of grammatical structures and vocabulary.

However, we need to bear in mind that readability is only one feature of text, which, as we saw in chapter 1, has severe limitations; these are discussed in greater detail in Davies (1986a) and (1993). There is also evidence that in their own reading, students frequently deliberately choose texts that are challenging for them to read. This suggests either that the acceptance of challenge is a means of learning and/or that other features of text are of greater importance to individual readers. None the less relative readability is an essential criterion for the selection of texts in the classroom.

3.2.2   Content

In both L1 and L2 contexts, content is principally determined by the requirements of the syllabus, but increasingly, particularly in L2 contexts, the criteria of interest and culture are influencing content selection. In all teaching contexts selection of content is clearly a basic consideration.

3.2.3 Affective response to text

As we saw in chapter 2, some researchers (Scott 1990, Oh 1990, Mathewson 1985) have begun to investigate ways of describing readers' affective response to different texts. Such research is in the very early stages. However, it is an area which can readily be investigated by teachers in their classrooms and may be predicted to be increasingly important as one way of describing different texts.

3.2.4 Rhetorical function

Texts have also been described through reference to their perceived rhetorical function and given descriptions such as 'persuasive', 'descriptive', 'expository' etc. Such labels do not refer to predicted difficulty or content, but to the broad social or communicative goals of the writer. Descriptions of text through reference to such goals not only seem to have some psychological reality but are also well-established in the field of rhetoric.

Brewer's framework for classifying texts (1980) is of particular interest as he not only identifies broad rhetorical functions but also relates them to real-world texts. In this he anticipates the broad theoretical framework developed by Halliday (1989) and Martin (1992). Davies (1990), building on Halliday's analysis, provides a classification that can be used as a basis for curriculum planning (see chapter 4).

3.2.5 Rhetorical patterns

In addition to broad rhetorical purposes, there are more specific 'lower-level' rhetorical labels such as 'cause–effect', 'comparison–

contrast', 'argument–exemplification', lists which are often used to describe short stretches of text. In contrast to the broad rhetorical, or goal-oriented rhetorical functions, these lower-level functions appear to identify the 'acts', devices, or means by which both general and specific social goals are achieved.

Amongst the **rhetorical patterns** identified to date are the 'matching' pattern (contrast and compatibility), 'general–particular' pattern (generalization–example and preview–detail), and the **problem–solution pattern** identified by Hoey (1983), whose patterns are based upon the analysis of a wide range of authentic texts. Similar labels are used by Meyer (1992), Meyer and Freedle (1975) and Meyer and Rice (1982), whose examples, by contrast with Hoey's, are derived from short, typically 'constructed' texts.

Like the more general rhetorical labels, the use of labels for describing rhetorical patterns is well-established in the classroom and is represented in influential guidelines for American teachers which have been developed on the basis of studies undertaken by Meyer and used, for instance, by Carrell (1984). In addition, the potential of the problem–solution structure, as illustrated by Hoey, is one pattern which has been widely used by teachers and for this reason is examined in detail in part 2 of this chapter.

3.2.6 Context: source of text

In recent years teachers have become increasingly interested in the potential of describing texts through reference to the context in which the text was produced and/or is read. One starting point for such a description of texts is to ask the question, 'Where has the text come from?' The notion of source provides the basis for a real-world perspective on texts and allows the teacher or researcher to be quite specific in giving an initial description of a text. For example, when we say that an extract comes from a geography textbook or an academic paper we are identifying its source. It is then possible to be even more specific in describing the social context and purpose of the text, for example, the context of secondary education, the process of introducing learners to geographical concepts and facts, and the relationship between the writer as 'informant' and the reader(s) as 'learners'.

A second reason for considering source and social context is that such an approach focuses attention on language variation, that is, the different kinds of language, or registers, that are selected by writers for different kinds of purposes. This provides a basis for studying the specific language choices, words, grammatical structures and so on that are associated with different social contexts and different kinds of texts.

The importance of the relation between a text and its social contexts is at the core of the functional theory of language developed by Halliday (Halliday and Hason 1985/1989) and his colleagues. According to Halliday: 'We can define text in the simplest way by saying that it is language that is functional. By functional we simply mean language doing some job in some context, as opposed to isolated words or sentences that I might put on the blackboard.'

Amongst the questions which Halliday and his colleagues seek to answer are, 'How can we characterize a text in its relation to its context of situation?' and, 'How can we characterize variation in texts through reference to the relationship between a text and its context?'

3.2.7 The concept of genre

It is in addressing such questions that Hallidayan linguists have introduced the concept of **genre** as a means of describing differences between texts and classes of texts. The definitions of genre used by Hallidayan linguists are in fact quite close to

Halliday's definition of a text: 'language doing some job in some context'. For Martin (1984), a genre is 'a staged, goal-oriented, purposeful activity in which speakers [or writers] engage as members of our culture.' Swales (1990) provides another definition which has been widely influential in the context of EAP/ESP teaching: 'genre comprises a class of communicative events the members of which share some set of communicative purposes.'

Despite the variation in wording in both definitions, the notion of purpose is critical. Note that both emphasize the process rather than the product of the communication and neither makes the notion of source explicit. These are points to which we will return when I discuss my own definition of genre.

3.3   Towards an integration of different descriptions of text

From the above it is clear that there are many ways of describing texts. The question thus arises, 'In what ways can such different perspectives be integrated?' In what follows and in Davies (1994a), I propose a hierarchy of levels of text as a practical framework for integrating these diverse descriptions.

3.3.1   A hierarchy of five levels of text

— discourse type
— genre
— text
— textual unit
— rhetorical pattern

Discourse type

In the proposed hierarchy, **discourse type** is the term which is given to descriptions of text through reference to the general rhetorical goals discussed above, e.g. description, exposition, persuasion, literary-poetic, didactic. Thus discourse type is defined as a class of genres. Such classes are rather abstract and indeed speculative, and hence discourse type labels can be applied to a very wide range of classes of text, or genres, and also to different parts of the same text. For most practical purposes however, it is more useful to think of discourse types as representing classes of genres.

Genre

We saw above that definitions of genre to date take account of social purposes and processes but that none make reference to source. The definition of genre in the proposed hierarchy builds upon both Martin's and Swales's definitions, with class and purpose as criteria for genre membership, but for practical purposes includes reference to source of text, thus recognizing genre as product as well as process. Thus a dual definition of a (written) genre is presented:
— genre as process: the staged goal-oriented social processes underlying a class of texts;
— genre as object: a class of (written) texts which reflect a particular set of social processes and goals and which derive from an identifiable and public source/environment, and which are directly or indirectly controlled by an 'editor' (see Davies 1988).

For example, publicity leaflets can be considered a genre with the social purpose of promoting a product etc, and this in turn can be described as the discourse type 'persuasive'.

From this definition it is clear that the purposes of genres, as represented here, are not only more public and institutionally oriented than the goals of discourse types, but are also directed at real-world audiences. In addition, the inclusion of the notion of source is intended to provide a real-world, testable criterion for the initial description of a text through the question: 'Where does the text come from?'

GENRE AND SOURCE ARE NOT THE SAME THING

However, it should be noted that the notion of source is not equated with genre, although genre and source may coincide. Thus at one level we can think of newspapers as a broad class of texts, or a 'genre' with the very broad social purpose of reporting and commenting on current events; however, since newspapers are made up of other classes of texts with varied and more specific social purposes, newspapers are at the same time sources in which more specific and clearly identifiable genres are represented, for example, editorials, letters to the editor, news stories etc. Such constituents of newspapers meet their criteria of genre membership much more clearly than does their source, the newspaper. By contrast, publicity leaflets pushed through the door are simultaneously source and genre.

GENRES AND PRE-GENRES

As for Swales, genres are distinguished from pre-genres. Pre-genres do not have a formal public status; rather they are writing which is either personal and private or which is 'apprentice', for example writing for the purposes of acquiring literacy rather than for publication. This distinction between published genres and pre-genres is important when selecting and using examples of genres in the classroom. As we shall see in chapter 4, it suggests that in planning a reading programme, a first question should be: 'What genres do my students need, or want, to read and to write?' and, 'What texts should I, or we, select as examples of the genres?'

Text

As we have seen, definitions of text vary, but in all, the notions of unity of texture and unity of structure are central. My research shows that readers can distinguish between complete texts and parts or units of text, which suggests that they have well-established ideas about the function of introductory and concluding sections of texts or books, and that writers give clear signals of what they are doing in introductions and conclusions. The criterion of completeness, therefore, is included in the following definition of text: a text is a coherent piece of writing exhibiting both structure and texture, assignable to a single author or collaborating authors, with clearly defined boundaries marking the beginning and end of the writing.

Clear-cut examples of complete texts thus include books, letters, brochures, annual reports etc. But the criterion of authorship also allows for articles within journals, magazines and newspapers, for example, editorials, letters to the editor, and chapters of books by different authors, to be counted as complete texts. Conversely, and in line with our intuitions, sections of an academic paper and sections of chapters of books cannot be counted as complete texts.

It is such units or sections of written discourse which are predicted to comprise the elements of structure of texts. These are located at the next level of discourse, that of **textual units**.

Textual units

A textual unit is defined as a part of a complete text that serves a specific communicative function within the text, which is reflected in the position it occupies within the text. In Davies (1994a and b), three types of textual unit are proposed and are seen to be related to Halliday's (1985) metafunctions of language as shown below:
—interactive units: predominantly though not exclusively concerned with negotiating the relationship between writer and

reader and hence expressing the <u>interpersonal</u> metafunction of language;
— organizational units, or linkers: predominantly though not exclusively concerned with linking one part of the text with another and hence with expressing the <u>textual</u> metafunction of language;
— topical or informing units: predominantly though not exclusively concerned with presenting information, and hence expressing the <u>logical/experimental or ideational</u> metafunction of language.

Rhetorical pattern

In the present account, rhetorical patterns are located at the lowest level of discourse and hence are hypothesized to be constituents of textual units. Thus a rhetorical pattern is defined as a communicative device for relating ideas in clauses or sets of clauses. A number of rhetorical patterns were identified above.

3.4   The levels of text most extensively studied

What should be noted about the five-level hierarchy is that it is the levels of textual unit and of rhetorical patterns that have been most extensively studied in research contexts. These are also the levels of text that are typically the focus of reading lessons and activities in the classroom. This is not surprising, since such units are of a length manageable in the course of a lesson. It will therefore be useful to examine examples of such units in greater depth.

3.4.1 Below the level of the text: examining textual units and their function

Terms like 'introduction' indicate first, an assumption about the position of textual units within a text and secondly, an awareness of the function of such units, for example, to introduce and contextualize the topic of the text. We will explore these ideas in greater depth by looking closely at two different textual units from the same text.

ACTIVITY

The two texts for analysis are presented on pages 96–7. Before undertaking the analysis you should note that both texts are taken from the same source and are also from the same broad genre. However, the two extracts are from different sections of the text and from this it may be predicted that they may be serving different functions. Your answers to the questions should throw some light on this. The questions you are asked to consider are:

— from what source are the two extracts drawn, and what genre do they represent?
— what is the broad social purpose of the genre, for example, to persuade consumers to buy, to inform the tax payer about procedures, to warn staff and students that there is construction work going on?
— who has written the text, and what role(s) is he or she adopting towards his or her readers, for example, 'friendly/equal/knower of secrets/reassuring expert', as in the advertisement 'concerned but distanced administrator', as in the official notice, or 'authoritarian and distanced civil servant', as in the tax form?
— what position in the original text does each extract occupy?
— what function in the text does each extract serve?
— what kind of language choices can you find to support your

judgements and in particular to distinguish between the two extracts?

3c

Because Liverpool is a major city, you will probably have heard something about it, even if you have never been here. Perhaps you think of it as 'the home of the Beatles', 'a major seaport', 'where the Grand National is run', or 'famous for Liverpool and Everton Football Clubs'. Liverpool is all these things, but it is also much more. This section sets out to show some of the features of Liverpool and the surrounding area which make it an attractive place to spend your student days. The next few paragraphs will tell you a little about sport and entertainment, local attractions, enjoyment further afield, shopping, food and drink and the Liverpool people.

Sport and entertainment

If Liverpool does mean music or sport to you, then you will not be disappointed. You can be part of the crowd at Anfield or Goodison Park, where you will see soccer of the highest quality: no other city has such a record of success in League and Cup competitions. What could be more alive than these grounds when the first team is playing at home? Some would say 'Aintree in April', for when the Grand National steeplechase takes place, the northern outskirts of the city teem with cosmopolitan life. But while these are the well-known sporting images of Liverpool, adherents of other sports will also have little difficulty in satisfying their needs.

3d

Liverpool is one of the minority of cities distinguished by two cathedrals. The Roman Catholic cathedral is almost on the Precinct. Visit it preferably on a sunny day, when the light streams through the stained-glass lantern into the vast interior. Irreverently nicknamed 'Paddy's Wigwam' or 'the Mersey Funnel', it uses modern stressed-concrete engineering to achieve its 'space capsule' outline and a spacious serenity within. The Anglican cathedral is built in the traditional way using masonry, and in sheer size it is the climax of the neo-Gothic style of building. The style is severe but not heavy; as in the finest medieval buildings, the huge stone arches seem to soar weightlessly into the great height above the nave. In typical Liverpool fashion, the Anglican cathedral was designed by a Roman Catholic and the Catholic cathedral was designed by a Protestant. Hope Street, aptly named, runs directly between the two cathedrals.

In the heart of the city centre is a gem of a seventeenth-century building called the Bluecoat Chambers (picture, page 189), which remains a haven of peace in the busy shopping area. Paintings by local artists are often displayed on its railings. For more formal exhibitions try the Walker Art Gallery, with the largest collection of paintings outside London, ranging from early Flemish to twentieth-century. The Tate Gallery Liverpool, which attracted 750,000 visitors in its first year of opening, houses a major collection of contemporary and modern art. It is situated in the Albert Dock, one of the best examples of Victorian maritime architecture still extant. In 1984 it was reopened as a social and business centre, and it now houses an exciting array of shops, restaurants and exhibition halls. The loving restoration has won many prestigious awards. Adjacent to the Albert Dock is the Maritime Museum, which makes the history of Liverpool shipping come alive; if you are lucky on the day you visit, you may see how barrels or ropes were made in the old days of sail, and at all times you can see examples of the boats which have served Liverpool down the years. The world-famous ferries are still a live Merseyside attraction. Across the river, the model village of Port Sunlight houses the Lady Lever Art Gallery, which contains one of the best collections of applied art in Britain.

The Halls of Residence have their own spacious grounds in the leafy suburbs. Nearby is Sefton Park, the largest municipal park in the country where you can walk, cycle, jog, or simply sit back and admire the surroundings.

(Liverpool University Undergraduate Prospectus 1991)

Identifying the source and genre of the units

On the basis of your analysis you were probably able to predict that the source of the two extracts was either a tourist guide or a tourist promotion leaflet; if you were more specific you might have identified the actual source, an undergraduate prospectus for Liverpool University. Whatever source you predicted, it is likely that you correctly identified the broad, social purposes of the writer, to 'sell, persuade, or promote' and also to 'inform', and would also have distinguished between the more specific purposes of each extract in some ways.

Examining writers' social and communicative goals

Thus, in the first introductory section, we see the writer doing a number of things which are aimed at achieving the broad social goal of persuading and the more specific goal of promoting a particular university and its city:
— signalling the overall topic of the text: Liverpool;
— establishing a real-world context within which to consider the topic: *Because Liverpool is a major city*;
— acknowledging the different expectations that different readers may bring to the text: *You may think of it as . . .*;
— signalling the organization of the text and the writer's goals: *This section sets out to show . . . The next few paragraphs will tell you about . . .*;
— identifying the sub-topics of the text: sport and entertainment, local attractions, further afield, food and drink, shopping and the people of Liverpool.

In these last two organizing functions we can also see that the writer is in some way making a promise. If we could see the complete text we would see that in fact the promise is fulfilled: the sub-topics of the complete text are all covered and they are dealt with in the order promised, starting with *sport and entertainment* and ending with *the people of Liverpool*. Furthermore, each sub-topic is clearly signalled through a subheading.

We can also see that in doing these 'introductory' things, the writer takes on the role of friendly informant who knows the city, but who is also familiar with the audience. At the same time he or she assigns potential roles to the reader, for example that of 'potential student at Liverpool', 'follower of sport, music or theatre', 'knower about marine history' etc.

From the above it should be clear that an analysis of social purpose, roles etc is in essence an analysis of the rhetorical functions of a text. However, unlike analyses of general rhetorical functions, it is based on the analysis of the real-world process of reading as an interaction between writer and reader. As such it is able to reveal in some detail the precise nature of this real-world interaction.

Language choice as a reflection of communicative purpose

However, what should be noted is that it is the language of the text that tells us about the functions of the text. What then are the language choices here that tell us what is 'going on'?

CHOICE OF SENTENCE-INITIAL ELEMENTS

Perhaps the most obvious of the language choices is that of the choice of elements in first position in the sentence or clause. In modern grammar this is technically referred to as the **theme** of the sentence or clause. In text **3c** the theme choices include reference to the reader and his or her potential circumstances and/or interests: *You*, *some* [of you], *adherents of other sports*, *If Liverpool does mean music or sport to you*; and reference to the writer/text: *This section, The next few paragraphs*. There is also the choice of the question form: *What* [do you think] ... From such choices it is immediately clear that here the writer is not only interacting directly with the reader, but also offering the reader a range of possible optional roles as a potential 'client'.

By contrast with this introduction, the choice of sentence-initial elements in text **3d** does not identify the 'participants' in the discourse, the writer and the reader, as in the introduction, but rather <u>entities</u> in the real world, the cathedrals, the parts of the cathedrals, other buildings of architectural interest etc. From this the informing role of the extract is evident.

In further contrast with the first extract, here the writer does not appear to feel the need to negotiate his or her role or to specify a role for the reader. Instead, the informing role seems to be taken for granted. This is not surprising in view of the fact that this role of informing was negotiated in the introduction: *This section will show . . ., The next few paragraphs will tell.* With this goal established in the introduction, the writer is thus free in the main body of the text to concentrate on informing.

CHOICE OF VERBS

The choice of verbs in text **3c** also helps suggest interaction between reader and writer; thus the verbs refer to the mental processes of perception and thinking: *hear, think,* and to verbal process: *tell* and *show.* In addition, the writer's goals are revealed through the choice of verbs of intention followed by the infinitive form of the verb, *sets out to show,* or through the choice of a 'future' verb, *will tell.* Such choices clearly reflect the writer's intention to initiate a dialogue with the reader.

By contrast the verbs in text **3d** are predominantly verbs describing actions or states: *uses, is built, was designed, houses, was reopened, runs, are displayed, is severe, is a gem, is situated.*

Cohesion

In these texts we can also see how the selection of certain related words contributes to the overall function of other texts. This feature of relations between words is known as **cohesion**. In essence the feature of cohesion derives from the fact that there is a range of different ways in which words are related to each other to create meaning and establish links and connections across sentences. Such relations are seen to be essential in contributing to the coherence and overall 'texture' of a text. For example, pronouns are related to the names of the characters to whom they refer, for example, she = Hasan, he = Halliday. This is an example of grammatical cohesion and is classified as reference. A very wide range of other examples of reference and other types of grammatical cohesion are discussed in detail in Halliday and Hasan (1976 and 1985/89).

LEXICAL COHESION

In addition, Halliday and Hasan provide an introduction to lexical cohesion. Lexical cohesion includes relations like collocation, the tendency of certain words to occur together, for example, 'chips' with 'fish'. Equally important in the context of teaching are the **lexico-semantic relations** of:

— equivalence, which is the relation of words being equivalent in reference or meaning to other words, for example, settee = sofa;
— the relation of opposition which is the relation of being opposite, or opposed in meaning, for example, cold/hot;
— inclusion which, in general terms, is the relation of one word/ entity being a part of a broader class, for example, flower– daffodil etc.

In informing sections of text, the relations of equivalence and inclusion are clearly marked. In text **3d** the relation of equivalence is expressed through selection of the grammatical cohesion tie of pronouns; in other cases through repetition. By contrast, the lexical cohesion relation of inclusion is expressed through the selection of those that refer to parts or features of Liverpool city and in particular of the city's buildings.

From the above it should be clear that the analysis of cohesion can provide a starting point for teachers interested in promoting language study and vocabulary development. In addition, as we shall see below and in chapter 4, analysis of the 'information structure' of texts and textual units provides a content-oriented entry point to texts and is closely related to the study of cohesion.

3.5   The theoretical basis of the analytic procedure

Against the background of this description of texts we need at this point to consider the relationship between the analytic procedures which have been used to study the texts above, and the theoretical concept of register, which for Hasan, is seen to provide the foundation for a description of different genres (Halliday and Hasan 1985/89). In order to show this relation we need first to consider the questions upon which our study of the texts has been based:
— what is the text about?
— where has it come from?
— what are the broad social purposes of the text?
— who wrote the text?
— to whom is the text addressed?
— what role(s) does the writer adopt?
— what role(s) does he or she assign to the reader?
— how is the text organized?
— what is distinctive about the language choices of the text?

3.5.1   Questions for the classroom

The above questions are practical and applicable to all types of text. In chapter 4 we will see that the questions have direct application in the classroom at all levels and contexts of education. We must also note that they are very similar to the questions developed by the LINC project (Carter ms) as a starting point for reading a text.

3.5.2 The notion of register

From the above it is also clear that the questions are of three basic types: questions about the content and purpose of the text, questions about writer/reader interaction and questions about the language of the text. These relate very closely to the three constituents of **register** which Hasan identifies: field, tenor and mode.

— the field specifies the social activity and goals that the text represents, for example, selling a product as in an advertisement;
— the tenor identifies the relationship between the writer of the text and his or her readers, for example, persuasive promoter of product to consumer;
— the mode identifies the language choices of the text, for example, those of the informal, spoken style, as in a personal letter, or of the more formal written style.

ACTIVITY

With the framework for describing texts which has been developed above you will find it informative at this point to select at least one or two course books, reading workshops or textbooks aimed at the students you teach. Study the reading material presented in the books and consider:

— whether or not the source of the material is made clear and whether or not there is any discussion of the context in which the text was produced;
— whether or not the reading material provides experience of both complete texts and different types of textual units;
— whether the textual units appear to be predominantly informative or whether they tend to be more interactive;
— whether the function of the different texts or units is signalled;

—in what ways different functions are signalled; in doing so do not ignore visuals of different kinds.

When you have done this try to make contact with a teacher who works in a completely different teaching context from your own and see if you can compare your findings, and consider the implications for teaching.

PART 2: INTRODUCING DIFFERENT ANALYTIC SYSTEMS

3.6 Analysing writers' communicative moves

One analytic system which has been widely influential in the field of EAP/ESP is the analysis of the communicative or rhetorical **moves** made by writers as they seek to 'persuade' their readers of the importance of what they are saying. Thus Swales (1981, 1990) identifies the different 'moves' and 'steps' made by writers in the introductions to their research papers in academic journals, for example, <u>establish a research territory</u>, <u>establish a research niche</u>, <u>occupy a research niche</u>. From these labels we can gain some idea of the social context in which research articles are produced. The extended framework termed CARS (Create a Research Space) developed by Swales provides students with substantial support for reading and writing in a research context.

In other contexts, of course, writers also seek to persuade, particularly in 'interactive' and 'organizing' units of text or in complete texts such as advertisements which are principally persuasive. From Swales's pioneering work, the concept of writer moves is one which can be adapted and applied to a range of texts in different contexts. Consider for example, the moves which might be made by a consumer writing a letter of complaint to a manufacturer or retailer, and the company's response to such a letter, or a journalist reporting good news or success stories in a local paper.

3.7 Analysing predominantly informative units of text

By contrast with Swales's focus on communicative moves, information structure analysis developed by the Reading for Learning Project (see Lunzer *et al.* 1984, Davies and Greene 1984) is concerned predominantly with informing units of text, and in particular with texts in subject areas in the school curriculum.

3.7.1 Analysing the information constituents of textual units

The analysis started with the intuitive categorization of informing units of text from across the curriculum which appeared to 'have some features in common'. The analytic process involved a trial and error procedure of labelling sections of authentic texts with reference to the kinds of information which appeared to be dealt with in each text/category of texts. As analysis proceeded, it became possible to allocate such types of information to the slots of an information constituent framework.

Information constituents in the topic-type physical structure

For example, in texts describing a physical structure, like the tooth structure text in chapter 1, the evidence indicates that four constituents are consistently found:

— parts of the structure
— location of the parts
— properties of the parts
— function of the parts

From this we can see that different types of topic may be identified through reference to their information constituents. For example, simple descriptions of such different topics as 'suspension bridge', 'flowering plant', 'microwave oven' etc. all contain references to parts, location, properties and function, and are thus classified as examples of the **topic-type**: physical structure. If you study the Tooth Structure text introduced in chapter 1 you will be able to identify the four information constituents of this physical structure topic-type.

Information constituents of the topic-type process

An information structure analysis of a different topic-type, process, is presented below.

Although rocks may not be soluble in water, nevertheless the wind, rain, and frost may break them up into smaller pieces. These are washed down by rivers and eventually reach the sea – maybe after many thousands of years – as mud, silt, and sand, which accumulate at the bottom of the sea, or in lakes. As the deposit gets thicker, the bottom part is squeezed more and more, and becomes a compact mass. Often the particles are actually cemented together through substances produced by chemical reactions. The shells of dead sea-organisms, which are made of calcium carbonate (or chalk), may form a layer on top of the mass, or at intervals between layers. Then the sea may have receded, or earth movements may have taken place, making the sea bed dry land. What was the sea-floor may now be hills or even mountain ranges. Rocks of this kind are called sedimentary rocks, and include limestone, chalk, sandstone and shales.

from Mee et al, *Science for the Seventies*

PROCESS TEXTS

State or form of phenomena	Time or stage	Property or structure	Instrument or agent of change	Action	Location	Transformation
Rocks		may not be soluble in water	wind rain frost	break up		into smaller pieces
These (smaller pieces)	eventually maybe after many thousands of years		rivers	wash down to reach	the sea at the bottom of sea or in lakes	as mud and sand accumulating
Bottom part of (accumulation)				is squeezed more and more becomes		a compact mass.
The particles (of compact mass)			substances produced by chemical reactions	cemented together		and
the mass		has a layer of shells on top or at intervals between layers				
sea-bed (or mass)			sea recession earth movement	dry seabed to make		
sea floor				becomes		
Rocks (hill and mountain ranges) are sedimentary rocks include limestone, chalk, sandstone, shales						dry land. dry land, hills, mountain ranges

(from Davies and Greene, *Reading for Learning in the Sciences*)

From this we can see that the information constituents that characterize a process topic-type are different from those of physical structure; however, it should be noted that the 'location' slot can occur in both topic-types.
— state or form of object/material
— location
— time or stage
— instrument or agent
— property or structure
— action

A range of different topic-types

However, this type of analysis is not restricted to descriptions of physical structures and processes, but has very wide application for the analysis of short stretches of texts which are predominantly informative rather than interactive. Some of the different topic-types that have been identified within this approach are presented in the table on page 110, together with the information constituents of which they are comprised.

This list is neither comprehensive nor exhaustive but it does represent many of the different topic-types found in subject text-books, particularly in secondary school and undergraduate text-books. The potential of topic-type analysis as the basis for the design of reading activities is illustrated in chapter 4.

3.8   Informing and interactive sections in the text

As we have seen, many texts are made up of a mix of informing and interactive units. The three texts from the Liverpool Under-graduate Prospectus we studied in part 1 of the chapter provided evidence that in some genres the three types of functional units are distributed as a sequence of sections or layers throughout.

Topic-type	Information structure constituents
Physical structure→	Part → Location + Property + Function
Process →	State or Form of Object/material → Location + Time or Stage + Instrument or Agent + Property or structure + Action
Characteristics →	Defining Features or Attribute → Tests/Measures of Data + Exemplar or Group
Mechanism →	Physical Structure → Action + Object/Material
Theory →	Hypothesis → Context + Text of Results + Interpretation
Principle →	Law or Principle → Conditions + Instances + Tests/Measures + Application of Principle
Force →	Source or Composition → Conditions + Instances + Tests + Effects
Instruction →	Step or procedure → Materials + Apparatus or Measure + Caution or Condition + Result + Interpretation
Social structure →	Member or Group → Location + Conditions + Role or Responsibility + Assets or Outcomes
State/Situation →	Participants → Conditions + Location (Time & Place) + Effects + or Innovation
Adaptation →	Species/Exemplar → Environmental Conditions/Effects + Adaptive Feature/Mechanism + Function
System/Production →	Producer or Production System → Product + Location + Requirement + Distribution

NOTES
Constituents immediately to the LEFT of the second arrow are OBLIGATORY and can be regarded as constants. Constituents to the RIGHT of the arrow are optional. They can be regarded as the variables which define the obligatory constituents. Conditions for optionality are assumed, but no predictions are made about what these are.
+ indicates 'and' not order.
The list given here is not assumed to be either exhaustive or definitive.

However, in some genres, particularly those consisting of short texts, for example, news stories, letters to the editor etc, a closer interweaving rather than a sequencing of the functional units might be predicted. One such example, originally taken from a *New Scientist* article describing a new invention, is presented below:

3e

(1) (a) Helicopters are very convenient for dropping freight by parachute, (b) but this system has its problems. (2) Somehow the landing impact has to be cushioned to give a soft landing. (3) The movement to be absorbed depends on the weight and the speed at which the charge falls.

(4) Unfortunately most normal spring systems bounce the load as it lands, sometimes turning it over. (5) (a) To avoid this, Bertin, developer of the aerotrain, has come up with an air-cushion system (b) which assures a safe and soft landing. (6) It comprises a platform on which the freight is loaded with, underneath, a series of 'balloons' supported by air cushions. (7) These are fed from compressed air cylinders equipped with an altimeter valve which opens when the load is just over six feet from the ground. (8) The platform then becomes a hovercraft, with the balloons reducing the deceleration as it touches down.

(9) Trials have been carried out with freight-dropping at rates from 19 feet to 42 feet per second. (10) (a) The charge weighed about one and a half tons, (b) but the system can handle up to eight tons. (11) At low altitudes freight can be dropped without a parachute.

(Hoey 1983)

ACTIVITY

Your task in analysing this text is to see if you can identify one section of the text which appears to more clearly concerned with informing than interacting with, or orienting, the reader.

When you undertook this analysis it is likely that the section you marked as informing was the section beginning at sentence 6 and continuing to the end of the text; however, in doing this task, you may have felt that this section was not the only section that was informative. Indeed you may have felt, 'Well it's all informative.' This is of course true. As we have seen, it is a basic axiom that every language expression has the primary function of informing. However, certain units of language appear to do more than simply inform.

3.8.1 The function of the introductory section

The first sections of this text, I suggest, are doing more than informing. Thus in the 'introduction', the text opens by informing the reader of the current situation in respect of freight dropping, and in doing so, provides a background or real-world context for what is to follow; it then goes on to outline the problem(s) associated with current systems, thus providing a motivation for what follows, that is, a positive response to the problem, which in itself serves not only to inform, but also to arouse the reader's interest in the description of the system itself.

3.8.2 The distribution and function of evaluation

Throughout this introduction there is clear evaluation, which initially is positive: *Helicopters are very convenient*, but which, with the statement and elaboration of the problem, becomes negative: *this system has its problems ... Somehow has to be cushioned Unfortunately ... bounce the load ... sometimes turning it over.* This negative evaluation then provides the context within which the positive response can be introduced: *Bertin ... has come up with ... assures a safe and soft landing.* In this way, I suggest, the introductory section serves to orient or prepare the reader for the quite technical description of the system in the rest of the paragraph.

This informing section, I suggest, is very different from the introductory section in that in it there is no attempt to orient or contextualize new information, nor is there any evaluation. Rather the text appears to be a simple example of a description of a mechanism, with its references to parts and their function and to the action of the mechanism.

3.8.3 The problem–solution pattern

We can see from the above that to analyse this kind of text, a more rhetorically oriented analytic system would be required. Hoey (1983) has developed a system of this kind which has become widely known as the Problem–Solution pattern. The constituents of this pattern as indicated in the above discussion are:

— Situation
— Problem
— Response
— Evaluation
— Basis of evaluation

Hoey's analysis of text **3e** is shown below.

Section		
1a	=	Situation
1b–4	=	Problem
5a	=	Response
5b	=	Evaluation
6–8	=	Response
9–10a	=	Basis of Evaluation
10b–1	=	Evaluation

Because the problem–solution pattern is widely used in certain genres, it has been widely used in both L1 and L2 classrooms (see, for instance, Johns, A. 1988 and Mason 1992). In view of this you should study the language elements highlighted in the above discussion to become familiar with the kinds of signals of the different 'moves' or parts of the pattern. From this you can see also see the use of the rhetorical device of comparison–contrast which signals the shift between the positive evaluation in the description of Situation, and the negative evaluation in the Problem section.

What is also of interest is the absence of evaluation in the 'topical', Response section and the measurement-based evaluation in the Basis of Evaluation section.

Wide application of the problem–solution pattern

The genre on which Hoey initially based his analysis was the broad genre of the 'popular science magazine' and *New Scientist* in particular. But the problem–solution pattern is also found in other popular journals and in engineering reports. As Hoey suggests, it appears that the pattern has evolved as a reflection of real-world processes; in the case of engineering, for instance, the 'problem' is indeed the real-world <u>raison d'etre</u> of the professional, whose expertise is required for its solution. In the case of popular journalese, however, the reader is not aware of the problem; the writer must therefore introduce it as a contextual frame within which to introduce 'the facts'.

3.9 A well-established model of narrative structure

Hoey has also applied the problem–solution pattern to the analysis of the broad genre of (simple) narrative, the genre for which even young children will have a well-established schema by the time they start schooling. Another analytic system which perhaps reflects such schemata more directly than the problem–solution pattern is Labov's (1972) **narrative structure** which has been widely used in schools as the basis for developing reading and writing skills (see for example Couture 1986 and Cortazzi 1993).

– Abstract: what about?
– Orientation: who, when, where, why, what?
– Complicating action: then what happened?
– Evaluation: so what?

– Resolution: what was the outcome?
– Coda: signals return to the present.

However it should be noted that in Labov's original study the first and last of these elements of structure, Abstract and Coda, were elicited by the research context itself; thus the abstract was always a summary of the narrative given in response to the researcher's question, for example, 'What was the most important fight you remember?' as illustrated in 'Well, one, (I think) was with a girl.' Likewise, the Coda was a means of informing the researcher that the narrative was completed and a return to the here and now was required, as in 'That was one of the most important.'

In view of this, teachers and researchers applying the model to simple narratives typically make use of the central four elements only.

3.9.1 Labov's account of evaluation

For Labov, evaluation is the underlying reason for the narrative. He not only specifies Evaluation as a separate element of structure but also allows it to be a subsidiary element of all other elements. Thus evaluation is distributed throughout the narrative.

Labov identifies a number of different types of evaluation all of which have the effect of 'suspending the action', for example, quantifiers, repeated items, negatives, futures and modals, the use of questions and answers and the imperative form and different types of attributives.

As we shall see in chapter 4, the analytic system has proved to have considerable classroom potential, either as part of a reading programme in which students are encouraged to search for structure, or as part of a writing programme in which students can learn to evaluate whether or not they have included all elements of structure, and in what way they have 'filled out' elements.

3.9.2 An extension of Labov's model

In such programmes many teachers have found it helpful to add to Labov's criteria. One of these additional features is evidence of participant goals as part of the Orientation section, for instance. The notion of goals is of course entirely consistent with a Hallidayan theory of language and text, and has been incorporated into psycholinguistic descriptions of story structure (Thorndyke 1977). It is, indeed, participant goals which give the narrative its shape and motivation. Furthermore, goals are clearly recognizable through their expression in very simple language forms, for example, the selection of a verb of intention or desire, such as, *he planned to outwit the enemy*, *she was determined to win the race*, together with the use of the infinitive, or through the selection of a named goal, for example, my *aim* in this paper is *to outline* . . . his *intention was to complete* the thesis by Easter.

SUMMARY

- Traditionally descriptions of texts have focused on readability, content and general rhetorical function. Rhetorical patterns have also been used as a description of texts in psychological experiments.
- In this chapter attention has also been drawn to more socially oriented ways of describing texts; at an informal level the potential of affective response to text is suggested.
- More formally, descriptions of text based on the concepts of genre and register as developed by Hallidayan linguists are seen to have potential for illustrating the importance of the social contexts in which texts are produced and read.
- However, definitions of text, text-type and genre vary widely.
- In an attempt to integrate different perspectives, a hierarchy of five levels of (written) discourse is proposed: Discourse Type, Genre, Text, Textual Units, Rhetorical Patterns.

- The hierarchy is seen to provide a basis for the selection of reading materials in the classroom and for describing the texts used in research studies of reading.
- The potential of different methods for analysing the structure and patterning of different types of written material is illustrated and specific analytic systems such as the analysis of author moves, information structures, problem–solution patterns and narrative structure are seen to have potential as the basis for designing active reading tasks for the classroom.

4 Designing a reading programme and reading activities

In this chapter we are concerned with the practical task of designing reading programmes and activities for the classroom. The chapter focuses in turn on the following topics:
— setting course objectives
— investigating student needs and perceptions
— selecting texts
— identifying reading purposes
— identifying different types of reading
— designing reading activities.

In doing so, the chapter seeks to place reading and the teaching of reading within the context of the broader curriculum and the day-to-day constraints under which many teachers work, including those of the coursebook or materials that are available in the classroom.

4.1 The place of reading in different curricular contexts

In previous chapters, and particularly in chapter 1, we have seen something of the range of different curricular contexts in which reading takes place and within which teachers seek to encourage effective reading. A brief review indicates that such contexts include:
— the infant/primary L1 classroom in which the major focus of the curriculum is developing the acquisition of literacy;

— the junior/middle school L1 classroom where extensive reading and reading for learning are encouraged;
— the middle/secondary L1 school in which teachers across subject areas are committed to collaborating in furthering reading for learning;
— the L2 language classroom wherein reading is one of the four skills being taught;
— the EAP/ESP classroom where reading for specific purposes may be the central or only language skill being taught.

From the above it is clear that although reading is important in all of the different contexts, the specific goals of reading instruction in each context will be subtly different. This variation is reflected in the section below which outlines possible course objectives for those different teaching contexts.

ACTIVITY

Select the set of objectives that most nearly corresponds to the group of learners you typically work with and use it, ideally with a colleague, as a framework for evaluating a course you are currently required to teach, or as the basis for planning a new course. Consider whether there are objectives in the framework that are not included in the course you are evaluating. Are there objectives in the course that are not included in the framework? What are the implications?

4.1.1   Setting course objectives: criteria for the design of a reading programme

For infant L1

Does the programme:
— provide the opportunity for the learner to activate and use top-down information and strategies including prediction as a bridge

to acquiring knowledge of the visual and grapho-phonic rules of written language;

— specifically provide the opportunity for the learner to draw upon spoken language competence, knowledge of grammar, lexis and phonology as a bridge to the interpretation of the meanings encoded in written text;

— allow the learner to draw upon existing schemata, particularly on the schema for narrative;

— encourage the growth of awareness of spoken–written contrasts;

— motivate the learner to 'read' further;

— allow for recycling, repetition;

— incorporate rhyming and rhythm as an introduction to letter–sound correspondences;

— foster confidence and the feeling of achievement?

For junior L1:

Does the programme:

— provide the opportunity for the learner to increase his or her vocabulary and knowledge of the lexico-semantic relations that characterize written text;

— provide the opportunity for the learner to utilize and build upon existing schemata, including schemata for stories, instructions, descriptions, guides etc;

— introduce learners to a wide range of schemata, such as descriptions of physical structures, mechanisms, processes, social structures, arguments;

— introduce the learners to an increasingly wide range of registers and genres as exemplified for instance in: advertising, guides, letters of different kinds;

— provide opportunities for learners to interact with texts and with other readers;

— encourage the growth of awareness of spoken–written contrasts;

—introduce learners to the actualities of different contexts of texts, different writer purposes, different reading purposes;
—introduce students to models for writing different kinds of texts;
—foster confidence and the feeling of achievement?

For secondary language across the curriculum (LAC)

Does the programme:
—encourage growth of awareness of relation between text and context and the fundamentally public purposes of written language;
—involve explicit attention to reading purposes and strategies and to the need to vary reading strategy according to text and purpose;
—involve study of register in the range of genres required across the curriculum and beyond the curriculum;
—involve interaction with texts and other readers;
—involve explicit evaluation of a range of strategies for effective study;
—involve students in a discussion of the nature of the reading process;
—involve critical reading and appreciation of literary purposes and forms;
—ensure that students take increasing responsibility for their study reading and feel confident of the progress that they are making?

For EAP/ESP

Does the programme:
—cater for the specific shared and individual needs of different students;
—provide opportunity for students to draw upon well-established

schemata as top-down source of information for processing a wide range of texts and genres;
— involve students in defining purposes, selecting texts and setting targets;
— involve students in discussion and analysis of the nature of the reading process;
— allow for learners from different language and cultural backgrounds to proceed bottom-up in the early stages of study, paying attention to visual features of the written language and to lexis;
— encourage awareness of the relation between social context and text, and in particular of the nature of academic and professional discourse communities;
— encourage awareness of spoken–written contrasts;
— involve students in analysis and evaluation of different study strategies;
— ensure that students feel responsible for their study reading and confident of the progress they are making?

For EFL

Does the programme:
— focus on spoken–written contrasts;
— involve explicit discussion of the purposes and problems of reading in L1;
— provide opportunity for students to draw upon L1 language awareness and on top-down knowledge of different genres in L1;
— involve students in defining purposes and setting reading targets;
— allow for bottom-up processing and attention to vocabulary in the early stages;
— where languages are from the same family, utilize awareness of cognates and of false cognates;

— allow for progression and recycling;
— involve students in active analysis of texts and in analysis and evaluation of reading strategies;
— ensure that students gain increasing confidence in their ability to 'decode' the second language and feel confident about the progress they are making?

4.2   Investigating student perceptions and needs

In undertaking the task above, you may at times have found it difficult to make any firm judgement; for instance in considering whether the programme provides the opportunity to draw upon existing schemata, you may have been unsure what particular schemata your students do bring to the reading task. In other words, you may well have found that there were gaps in your own knowledge of your students; if you were able to work with a colleague you may have found that you were each able to contribute some ideas the other had not thought of. This suggests that there is always something more to be learned about the students we teach. This is certainly the view of most experienced teachers and researchers. And it is this that prompts many of them to undertake classroom-based investigations of their students' reading behaviour, strategies, needs, interests and knowledge and to monitor student progress regularly.

For many teachers a first priority in designing a reading programme is information about the different perceptions students bring to the learning task according to their language background, general background knowledge and interests, and about their expectations and strategies for reading and learning.

The investigation of such factors is seen not only to provide an important database for course planning, but the process of investigation itself is seen to play a critical role in initiating the 'dialogue' about reading and about texts which is a central part of any reading programme. The central role of talk, with both teacher and peers, as the basis for fostering positive attitudes to reading has always been recognized by L1 infant teachers; it has also been a key feature of many EAP/ESP programmes in the context of higher education worldwide (see, for instance, Scott 1986, Hedge and Gosden 1991, Swales 1981, 1990), and in an L1 curriculum, and is increasingly incorporated into EFL textbooks.

4.2.1 Potential areas of investigation

Here our focus is on ways of investigating students' needs, perceptions etc, not only as the starting point for classroom dialogue, but also as the basis of course design. A summary of possible areas of investigation is presented in the section below, together with possible examples, although it must be noted that the examples are not intended to be comprehensive. For this reason you are encouraged to supplement the list with examples of your own.

ACTIVITY

Ideally with a colleague, select from the table or from your own interests two broad areas for investigation, and consider ways in which these might be investigated. Then refer to chapter 1 to see if you get any further ideas.

Student perceptions of/attitudes to:

— purposes for reading in L1
— purposes for reading in L2
— demands for reading in L1/L2
— reading tasks included in current course materials
— texts in current reading course
— 'valued' texts in L1/L2

— difficult/unfriendly texts
— strategies for reading in L1/L2
— the target language and culture, for example, English culture, people, the country/other English-speaking countries.

Students' experience of/preferences for different genres

— instructional genres
— informative genres
    for study purposes
    for evaluation/assessment
— persuasive genres
— literary/poetic genres
    for study purposes
    for evaluation/assessment
— popular/entertainment genres
— social interaction.

Background knowledge/learning styles and study strategies

— background knowledge of specific topics, for example, local environment/community, national/international affairs, popular culture etc
— risk-taking/caution
— reliance on phonology/grammar
— reference to dictionary
— reference to other sources
— repetition/memorizing
— sequential read/reread
— selective non-sequential read
— sub-vocalizing/visualizing
— text marking
— construction/use of visual aids/tables
— question formulation

— awareness of context

— use of 'informants', for example, family, friends.

From the above it is clear that the range of possible areas of investigation is extensive and that it will not be practical for an individual teacher to attempt to investigate all areas at any one point. For this reason, the list should be regarded as a source of ideas from which individual teachers will select according to the profile of their learners and throughout a course of study. Thus an investigation of students' experience of different genres/texts may be the focus of an investigation at the early stage of a course, followed by a series of investigations of background knowledge and learning styles, while the monitoring of study strategies may be conducted at regular intervals throughout the course, and the investigation of student attitudes to different reading tasks may well be delayed until they have a comprehensive basis of experience of different tasks.

4.2.2   Selecting a methodology for investigations

Having selected your areas of investigation, the next step is to select a methodology. The section below outlines a range of possible methods of investigation. You and your colleague may have already identified one or more of these methods.

Methods for investigating reading purposes and tasks

— teacher-designed direct probe questionnaire, with option of follow-up interview to collect retrospective data;

— student-designed questionnaire and report-back to class with questionnaire revised on basis of feedback (option of recording);

— post-task, retrospective evaluation of different reading activities by students, through completion of questionnaire or through open-ended evaluation;

— collection of introspective data through recording of think-aloud or talk-aloud as students undertake a reading activity or problem-solving exercise either individually or in pairs/small groups.

Methods for investigating student experience of/preferences for different genres

— teacher-designed direct probe questionnaire, with option of follow-up interview to collect retrospective data;
— student-designed questionnaire and report-back to class, with questionnaires revised on the basis of feedback (option of recording);
— student identification and evaluation of extracts from different genres selected by teacher:
    students completing task in writing individually
    or working in pairs or small groups and reporting back
    and/or students talking aloud either individually or in groups
    with talk recorded on tape.

Methods for investigating background knowledge and strategy use

— teacher-designed direct probe questionnaire with option of follow-up interview to collect retrospective data;
— student-designed questionnaire with report-back to class and revision of questionnaire on basis of feedback;
— pre-task prediction of strategies that will be used for particular reading task, followed by post-task review of actual strategy use, ideally with recording of think-aloud of individuals or pairs working on task;
— teacher talk-through reading task and strategies during recorded interview with one or two students;

— student-student recorded talk-through during reading task for beginning readers in L1 and L2, miscue analysis;

— with more advanced L1 and L2 readers, and particularly for large classes, the analysis of recall protocols and of modified cloze responses, to investigate specific questions about the processing of different texts;

— for all groups, the use of prediction tasks and of think-aloud and retrospective protocols (oral or written) to elicit individual responses to different texts.

4.2.3 Factors to be considered in selecting a methodology

Purpose of investigation

In selecting a methodology, one factor to be considered is the purpose of the investigation: is your objective to gain a broad profile of the class, and/or of variation within the class, or is it to focus on the problems of one or two individuals whom you judge to need special help? Similarly, is the purpose of the investigation the serious exploration of a research question as it would be on an MA course or is it, at least in part, a means of initiating a dialogue about reading and text?

All objectives, of course, are legitimate, but each will have its own constraints. If the investigation is oriented towards formal research, then careful consideration will need to be given to the piloting and design of the questionnaire; if it is dialogue-oriented, considerations of time, simplicity and user-friendliness will be paramount.

Practical constraints: equipment

Another critical consideration is what equipment is available, for instance for recording. There is no doubt that recordings provide an invaluable tool, allowing time to replay, stop, reflect and review what is being revealed in think-aloud protocols. However, financial and timetable constraints will determine the amount of recording that is practically possible. So too, will size of class. It is for these reasons that the option of student-designed and conducted question-naires and interviews is included above. Such investigations are unlikely to yield valid research data (except about student percep-tions of the questionnaire and the area of investigation), but they will be highly effective in raising awareness.

It is against this background, then, that you should now be in a position to design two small-scale studies that should help you find out more about your students' perceptions and experience of differ-ent genres, different reading and study strategies, and perceptions of different reading tasks.

4.3   Selecting texts: identifying criteria for the selection of genres, texts and textual units

Here we address the question: 'What genres, what exemplars of each genre, what units of text, will form the basis of the reading programme?' In chapter 3 we saw that there is potentially a wide range of texts from which to select. This suggests that it is important for teachers to establish clear criteria for the selection of texts. A first criterion is type of genre. The table on pages 129–9 presents a classification of different genres through reference to the broad social function of the text to reader purpose.

ACTIVITY

Use both the broad categories and the examples of each genre in the table on pages 130–31 to analyse:
— the reading materials you are currently using;
— the reading materials your students select for their own purposes.

CLASSIFICATION OF GENRES WITH REFERENCE TO PRIMARY
SOCIAL FUNCTION AND READER PURPOSE

Instructional

Transactional genres intended to enable readers to do something, to take action,
to negotiate the real world.

- transport timetables
- safety notices
- laboratory and technical instructions
- manuals for domestic appliances
- the highway code
- computer and word-processor manuals
- instructions for popular indoor and computer games
- rule-books for standard outdoor games
- travel brochures
- advertisements for jobs
- job descriptions
- university and college brochures
- application forms
- institutional guide lines and regulations
- safety regulations

Informative

Transactional genres intended to, or with the potential to, enable pupils to study
and learn across the curriculum.

---

1 Genres for study purposes

- textbooks across the curriculum
- worksheets
- exam questions
- encyclopedias
- reference books
- dictionaries and thesauruses
- letters requesting information/ thanking people who have helped in a project
- primary source texts:
- charters
- old newspaper articles
- diaries
- academic papers
- film and theatre reviews
- biographies
- specialist journals.

---

2 Genres for evaluation/assessment

Genres pupils are required to gain control of through their study and writing in
the content areas of the curriculum.

- informative, coherent, well presented project reports
- transcripts of coherent, informative oral presentations
- informative, coherent lab. reports
- clear and accurate instructions for an experiment or set of observations
- clearly structured letters requesting information/thanking people/agencies

---

Persuasive

Genres directed at specific audiences (either narrow or wide), intended to
persuade readers to buy, to adopt a particular socio-political viewpoint, or to
take a certain course of action, necessarily requiring critical evaluation by those
audiences.

- printed advertisements of different kinds
- government and political party propaganda
- 'special offer' leaflets or notices
- letters to the editor in local and national newspapers
- newspaper reports from different newspapers
- transcripts of television news/radio programmes
- editorials
- transcripts of peer group persuasion

Literary/poetic

Genres developed within a literary tradition and intended to be evaluated either within the terms of reference of this tradition and/or those of the wider literary/social/political milieu of the period.

1 Genres for study
 fairy tales and fables
 myths and legends
 classic children's literature
 modern children's literature
 pre-twentieth-century novels, drama and poetry
 modern novels, drama and poetry
 'serious' science fiction
 the critical review/essay/social commentary
 literary criticism as exemplified in academic journals and books

2 Genres for evaluation/assessment

Literary/poetic writing exemplifying pupils' developing awareness of this broad genre.

 poems, stories and dramatisations written by pupils in class and/or of other age
 age groups, schools or countries

Popular/Entertainment

Genres evolved from, or for, the community and intended primarily as an expression of shared experience and/or for popular entertainmnent, distinguishable from literary/poetic genres only through the gradual development of appreciation of these forms together with the opportunity to critically evaluate the popular genres.

nursery rhymes	popular magazines
playground rhymes and riddles	comics
popular adventure	the detective novel
romantic novels	thrillers
historical romance	humorous fiction
science fiction	stories about animals

Social interaction

personal letters	FAX messages
postcards	greetings cards
notes	telegrams
memos	

Source: Davies F. (1990)

Then consider how you might extend or 'balance' the range of genres and texts in your reading programme. In doing so, make reference to the framework of course objectives to ensure that your criteria include those of language level, background, interest and needs of your students.

ACTIVITY

On the basis of the criteria you have established make a list of the basic genres/texts that you think will be appropriate for your student group. Then compare your list with that of a colleague. Consider whether this process makes you aware of additional criteria. As a next step, start to search for actual texts that are appropriate examples of those on your list. But note that this part of the task may take some considerable time spread over a number of weeks. As you undertake it you should also be considering the social context within which you located certain texts and the different purposes for which the text might be read.

4.4   Identifying reading purposes

Here we focus on the importance of purpose in private reading and the range of different purposes for which individuals read. There is evidence that there is a close relationship between reading purpose and text; reading for pleasure typically, though not always, determines the choice of a text that is narrative and or literary in style; reading for learning typically, though not always, requires the selection of a predominantly informative text. In addition, there is also a relationship between reading purpose and types of reading, for example, 'skimming', 'scanning', 'skipping', and 'getting the gist' (terms that will be reconsidered below), and different study strategies.

   This suggests that the discussion of reading purpose, like that of the social context of a text, should be an integral and explicit part

, classes, and that such discussion can be initiated
ase of simple questions, particularly when students are
h reading for their own study purposes. In order to
such questioning, a preliminary summary of different
purposes is presented below.

Reading purposes

For pleasure

— to follow a narrative
— to enjoy the 'sound' and rhythm or rhyme of a literary text.

For a general impression

— to gain an idea of the writer's viewpoint
— to gain an overall impression of the 'tone' of a text
— to decide whether or not to read the text.

For organizing reading and study

— to identify the important content of a text
— to answer a specific question(s)
— to decide which section of a text to start studying.

For learning content or procedures

— to gain an understanding of new concepts
— to learn certain facts from a text
— to follow instructions.

For language learning

— to 'translate' the text, literally or metaphorically
— to learn new vocabulary
— to identify 'useful' structures or collocations
— to use the text as a model for writing
— to practise pronunciation.

From the above, it is clear that there is a wide range of specific purposes for which we may read and that our specific purposes may change during the course of reading a single text. Thus the questions we ask our students to consider will vary according to both the nature of the text and the level and background of our students. The section above provides a source for the selection of questions for different groups of students and different contexts of study. It also provides a basis for considering the type of reading most appropriate for specific reading purposes.

When we are clear about reading purposes and text we should be in a position to consider the most appropriate type of reading to adopt. When reading for pleasure, a certain degree of 'skipping' can be tolerated; when reading in order to organize study, it is usually sensible to start by 'skimming' the text for key signals of content etc. But reading for the learning of content, or procedures, requires slower reading, reading in depth, and time for reflection. Reading for learning the language will require a combination of strategies in sequence.

Unfortunately these simple principles are ignored in many text-books, particularly in EFL where the predominant exercises are aimed at 'getting the gist' and/or at the skimming and scanning of texts which, by their very nature, need to be read carefully.

In view of the pervasive influence of such exercises, it is important at this stage that we examine the terms commonly used to describe such reading activities both in coursebooks and in the research literature.

4.5   Identifying different types of reading

In the research literature, two broad categories of overt response to text are distinguished: reading strategy, and **type** or **style of reading**. The first category refers to spontaneous learner behaviours such as those reported in chapter 1. The second category, with which we are concerned here, includes the different behaviours that students are encouraged to practise in the reading classroom such as scanning, skimming, skipping and less well-known types of reading such as 'receptive' and 'reflective' reading, or a 'smooth read', an 'item read', a 'search read' etc.

While it is beyond the scope of this volume to review the literature on these types of reading, it is necessary for our present purposes to establish a basic terminology. In order to do this, here I draw upon and amplify the types of reading behaviour identified by two authorities on reading, Lunzer and Gardner (1979) and Harri-Augstein and Thomas (1984). The methodology used by Lunzer and Gardner was classroom observation. By contrast, the methodology used by Harri-Augstein and Thomas involved a reading recorder, which produces a record of the pauses and regressions of individual readers reading a script at their own pace. From such records, and from interviews with subjects after reading, Harri-Augstein and Thomas have identified five distinct 'patterns' of reading, or 'reads', as shown on page 136 that are associated with different levels of performance or measures of comprehension.

Together the Lunzer and Gardner and Harri-Augstein and Thomas studies provide a basis for a categorization of the types of reading behaviour that can be used by both the classroom teacher and the teacher/researcher as follows:

— receptive reading, which characterizes the smooth, fluent, apparently unconscious ('escapist'), reading of a narrative, and which, according to Lunzer and Gardner, is 'the most familiar and approximates to listener behaviour'. This 'style' of reading

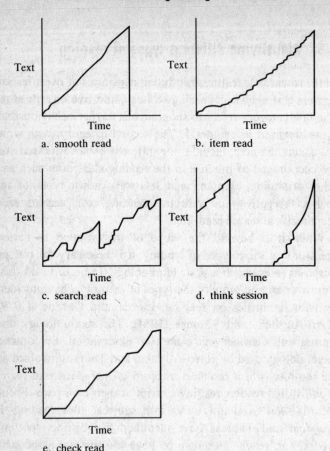

a. smooth read

b. item read

c. search read

d. think session

e. check read

FIVE TYPES OF READ

Read (a) a fairly rapid, more or less smooth continuous read from beginning to end;

Read (b) a slow read from beginning to end with detailed hesitations and possibly notes;

Read (c) a read that shows considerable search backwards and forwards within the text;

Read (d) an activity associated with 'thinking', note consultation, drafting sessions and so on during which specific parts of the text may be consulted briefly;

Read (e) a fairly rapid read with a few hesitations at selected parts of the text.

appears to be analogous to the type of reading identified by Harri-Augstein and Thomas as a 'smooth' read.

— reflective reading, as defined by Lunzer and Gardner, 'is reading which is frequently interrupted by moments of reflection' and which is seen by Lunzer *et al.* (1984) and Davies and Greene (1984) to be an essential prerequisite for study reading and reading for learning. This style of reading appears to be analogous to two types of 'read' identified by Harri-Augstein and Thomas as the 'search read' and the 'thinking read'.

— skim reading 'is a rapid style used mainly to establish what a text is about before deciding where to read' (Lunzer and Gardner). On the surface, it appears to have some features in common with Harri-Augstein's and Thomas's category of 'search read', in that it involves 'considerable searching back and forth in the text'.

— scanning, according to Lunzer and Gardner, 'is a kind of skimming to see if a particular point is present in the text or to locate it'. In that it involves the checking of specific items and hesitations at selected parts of the text, it appears to embrace Harri-Augstein's and Thomas's 'selective check read' and their 'item check read'.

From the above, however, it will be clear that it is difficult to draw clear boundaries between the types of reading termed skimming and scanning; in real life, scanning inevitably involves some skimming (and skipping) of large sections of text, and skimming, reciprocally, must embrace some scanning. Furthermore, skimming and scanning both involve fairly rapid superficial reading and both are aimed at searching, rather than deep processing of the text or reflection upon the content of the text.

For these reasons, skimming and scanning are treated here as two different forms of a broader category, the search read. Within this category, they are distinguished by purpose; the purpose of skimming is to gain an overall impression of the text, that of scanning to locate specific items of information.

With this distinction established we can now identify four different types of read: receptive reading, reflective reading, search read/skimming, search read/scanning.

4.5.1 Two additional types of reading

Listen read

For our present purposes, I would also wish to add two further types of reading, neither of which is addressed by either Lunzer and Gardner or by Harri-Augstein and Thomas. The first of these is what I shall term as listen read: that of 'listening' to an oral reading of a text. As the term implies, a listen read involves readers in a stage of text processing that is either 'led', or accompanied by, an oral reading of the written text. This type of reading is one which has traditionally been used to provide support for beginners, but as we saw in chapter 2, is also seen to be helpful for those advanced learners who spontaneously resort to an oral rendering of text in certain circumstances. For students at all levels, it is also a basic route to the appreciation of the 'sound', rhythm and rhyme of literary texts, and a means of keying into grammatical structure and meaning through intonation.

Practice read

The second additional type of reading we will consider is the kind of read that many teachers will recognize as a 'plodding' read, a laborious, step-by-step struggle through the text, often accompanied by hesitations and back tracking. Such reading can often be observed at the beginning stages of reading in both L1 and L2 contexts. However, it is not confined to the beginning stages of reading and frequently reappears as a 'strategy' adopted by advanced readers when confronted with particularly demanding reading material, as for instance may have been your own experience when reading certain parts of this book. Here the term adopted for this plodding style of reading is that of the practice read.

Because of its laborious nature, practice reading is seen to indicate a problem in many classrooms; indeed in many EFL textbooks, such reading is regarded as a 'sign' of bad reading strategies and is treated as unacceptable. In such contexts, the typical remedy is to exhort students to skim, scan and read for gist as a means of avoiding plodding.

This is not the view taken here. Instead it is recognized that for some students at some points in their reading development there may be a need to engage in practice reading and that such reading may well be laborious and time-consuming. In such circumstances the teacher's role will be to help the student identify his or her reading purposes and the source of the difficulties encountered, and to monitor the strategies available for overcoming difficulties.

In the early stages of L1 reading the source of difficulty may be grapho-phonic or lexical; in L2 reading, it may be visual, for example, coping with an unfamiliar script, or syntactic; in the case of advanced readers the source of difficulty may be conceptual, or may arise from certain apparently familiar lexical items being used to represent unfamiliar meanings. In all contexts, the practice reader will inevitably be burdened by what Hedge (1991) has termed 'dual drivers', seeking simultaneously to gain access to both meaning and content and at the same time trying to learn about some aspect of the language system.

For this reason the practice read is a type of reading that must be recognized; as such it represents the final type of reading that will be illustrated in what follows. A summary of the six different types of read as they are related to reading purposes is presented below. It must be noted, however, that the apparently tidy categorization of types of reading as outlined above is in reality much more fluid: a read that may start as a skim-read can be suddenly halted by a particular section of text, which will then be read carefully and reflectively; similarly receptive reading may be alternated at frequent intervals by cycles of reflection.

— LISTEN READ as a route to either RECEPTIVE or REFLECTIVE READING for the purposes of pleasure and learning about text structure and the relation between print and speech;
— PRACTICE READ involving slow, hesitant text processing aimed at the understanding of content but also requiring conscious attention to lower-level orthographic or lexical or syntactic features of text, for the dual purposes of understanding in depth and learning about the language system;
— SEARCH/SKIM READ of the text for the purposes of 'getting the gist' and/or as a route to critical evaluation of texts;
— SEARCH/SCAN-READ to locate specific items of information for the purposes of organizing study reading;
— REFLECTIVE READING involving in-depth reading, pausing, regression and reflection on what is read for purposes of learning and appreciation;
— RECEPTIVE READING involving a smooth, typically unconscious reading of undemanding, familiar or narrative text, for pleasure and 'unconscious' language learning.

The reading activities outlined below are designed to illustrate the way in which different types of reading can be matched to different reading purposes and different texts. The basic assumption is that there is a place in the classroom for all of the different types of reading, that each serves different and important purposes and that none is inherently 'bad'. Thus it is recognized that at certain stages of learning, the slow, hesitant 'bottom-up' plodding of the practice read may be both unavoidable and necessary for further progress. Conversely, while skim and scan reading are seen to serve a number of useful purposes, they do not receive the emphasis that they do in many course- and skills books. Rather they are seen as necessary precursors to reflective reading, which is recognized as necessarily involving pausing and regression as part of in-depth processing of text.

It is thus important to keep in mind the purpose of the classification, that is, to ensure that students have balanced experience of the different types of reading and the opportunity to evaluate their potential for different purposes.

ACTIVITY

Despite the fact that you are not equipped with a reading recorder, you should be able to make an informal study of the different types of read you adopt in your own day-to-day reading. In order to do this, you should try to keep a record, over the period of a normal working week, of the different kinds of read you utilize, for example, the 'smooth read' of a novel, the 'search' or 'think' read for study purposes etc.

4.6   Designing reading activities

4.6.1   Contextualizing reading

We turn now from considerations of course design to the design of reading activities exemplifying the different types of reading that can be practised in the classroom. However varied, the activities have certain features in common. The first is that they are intended to be contextualized activities. In contextualized activities reading tuition is undertaken within a meaningful context of social interaction, illustrations and real discourse, as opposed to a decontextualized focus on language items out of context.

Here the notion of context is extended beyond the text to include a consideration of the social context of the text/textual unit under study and different reading purposes and different types of reading. In the classroom this implies that all reading lessons/activities are introduced and conducted within a context that involves explicit discussion of these aspects of reading.

The classroom procedures for raising student awareness of these factors build directly on the reports of readers' response to text reported in chapter 1. Translated into classroom practice, they constitute a series of questions that should always precede the study of any new text and that should also be reconsidered as part of the study of familiar texts. In brief, they involve the discussion of such simple questions as the following:

— where do you think the text has come from, for example, a book, a magazine, a leaflet, a letter etc?
— what kind of person might have written the text?
— what were the writer's purposes in writing the text?
— for what particular group(s) of readers do you think the text was written?
— what is my/our response to the text?
— what will be our purposes in reading the text?
— what type of reading and/or reading strategies will be appropriate for our purposes?

4.6.2 Active reading

In addition to being contextualized, the activities introduced are also designed to involve students in active, rather than passive, reading. At present there is no comprehensive analysis of the differences between active and passive tasks, but a preliminary categorization is presented below. This draws upon analyses of reading tasks presented in Davies and Greene (1982), Johns and Davies (1983), Scott (1986), Sheldon (1984), Davies and Greene (1984), and Swales (1990).

Passive reading tasks, typically involving individual silent reading:

— multiple-choice exercises
— comprehension questions
— gap completion exercises
— true/false questions
— vocabulary study, for example, find synonyms/antonyms
— dictionary study
— 'speed' reading
— renumbering of sections of text on page.

Active reading tasks, with targets and frameworks provided by the teacher and based upon the teacher's analysis of the text; typically students working in pairs/groups:

— marking/highlighting of text targets
— modified cloze
— diagram completion/construction
— table completion/construction
— labelling of text and/or diagram
— sequencing of cut-up units of text
— prediction.

Active reading tasks, students working individually, with 'framework' or guidelines provided by teacher:

— diagram/completion/construction
— table completion/construction
— review of book
— précis/summary
— recall
— note-making.

From the above, it is clear that active reading tasks represent a radical alternative to traditional comprehension and multiple-choice exercises. As we have seen, the validity of such comprehension exercises as measures of comprehension has been seriously questioned in recent years. More particularly such tasks are seen to have extremely limited potential as learning activities. By contrast with traditional comprehension exercises, active reading tasks:

— typically make use of authentic and challenging texts;
— contextualize reading;
— provide students with a rhetorical or topical framework for processing and analysing the text;
— frequently involve an oral reading of the text by the teacher or a student followed by silent reading and rereading of the text;
— involve students interacting with the text and each other;
— involve students in direct analysis of the text instead of indirect question answering;
— frequently involve the transfer of information from text to a visual or diagrammatic representation.

As a consequence of these features, active reading tasks change the nature of students' interaction with texts in the following ways:

— students make their hypotheses explicit;
— hypotheses are evaluated by other students and checked against the text;
— there is discussion about alternative interpretation;
— students ask questions about what they do not know instead of answering questions to which they know the answers or which may be seen to be irrelevant;
— if necessary, the teacher can adopt a rule of informant rather than that of inquisitor;
— students learn to be critical in their reading of a text.

4.7 Activities to encourage different types of reading

4.7.1 Encouraging reading for pleasure: listen read with search read

This first activity is not original; indeed it is probably the most fundamental of the reading activities of the L1 primary classroom. Here it is recommended as an integral part of the EFL classroom. In the beginner or EFL classroom, it takes as its starting point the power, or indeed compulsion, of the narrative and the poetry of language and simply exploits these, first through an oral reading of the text, with listeners following the written text, and secondly through a search for central aspects of the narrative, for example, the setting and the characters' goals, the complicating action, and the possibilities of resolution and, subsequently, evaluation.

Thus students are provided with a preselected photocopied extract from the narrative and follow the oral reading of the extract. They then work in pairs or small groups exploring one or more aspects of the narrative by seeking answers to questions such as:
— where and when does the story take place?
— who are the main characters?
— what are they like, and how do you know?
— what are the goals of the main characters, and how can you tell?
— how will they be achieved?
— what kind of resolution do you predict?

In answering questions students should be encouraged to identify (ideally by marking copies of extracts) the parts of the text they have used in answering the questions; these 'clues' can range from the use of capital letters for names of characters, to the identification of infinitives and verbs of intention/desire that realize goals, as in *the old farmer was trying to put the donkey in its shed*.

In more advanced classes, the use of an oral reading of a text also has potential and need not be confined to narrative. As a first step towards more directed reflective reading, a listen read of an editorial, for instance, can exploit the potential of intonation as a signal of evaluation and also help listener–readers gain a feel of complex grammatical structures.

4.7.2   Practice read

In the second type of activity, the practice read, the focus is on the individual reader and his or her individual response to the text and in particular on the strategies the student uses for dealing with difficulties in processing. As we saw in chapter 2, the evidence demonstrates that the utilization of specific strategies varies widely across individuals and is not, in reality, under the control of the teacher.

For this reason, the aim of the teacher in the practice read class should be to raise student awareness of the range of different sources of information and strategies that may be useful and to help them learn to monitor and evaluate their own utilization of such sources of information. Such monitoring must necessarily be aimed at achieving some trade-off between predicting and searching for meaning, and treating the text as an orthographic/linguistic object. The problem for the student is that time is required for visual/orthographic and lexical processing, but too much attention to such detail, for example, checking words in a dictionary, will interrupt the construction of meaning. But it is only the student, not the teacher, who can ultimately control this trade-off and who can monitor his or her processing of the text.

This does not mean that the teacher cannot provide support, but rather that the teacher's role should be facilitatory rather than prescriptive. A first step in fulfilling this role is the explicit recognition of the problems students have to solve; the second is to create some space in the classroom for students to engage in practice reading, and the third is to initiate an ongoing dialogue about strategies for solving the problem.

In the long term, practice reading is most appropriate for use with student-selected texts, that is, texts students need or want to read. However, in introductory sessions aimed at initiating dialogue and encouraging self-monitoring, the text(s) should be selected by the teacher and should be sufficiently demanding to stretch students and to activate a practice or plodding read. This will ensure that the initial discussion is based on shared experience. And in view of the fact that practice-reading classes involve difficult reading, the texts used in initial sessions in all classroom contexts should either be extracts from 'classic or mainstream' fiction, as in L1 or L2 beginning reading, or informative textual units, as in LAC, EFL intermediate/advanced reading or EAP; as students gain confidence, interactive/orienting textual units can be introduced.

The introduction to the lesson should involve students in reflecting upon and thinking about their reading purposes, different types of reading and their experience of practice reading and the strategies they use to improve their efficiency. The aim should be to illustrate and exemplify strategies that may have potential for this purpose, and will subsequently be evaluated. Thus amongst the possibilities that should be considered in discussion are:

— how can we use previous knowledge in reading the text?
— what do we already know about this topic?
— what could be key concepts, and how might they be worded?
— what types of words will I need the dictionary for, and which should I try to infer from context?
— what sources of information are available to help me in the classroom?
— should I skim/scan in advance for useful clues or for difficulties?
— will I find it helpful to read aloud at some points, to mark the text, to use a dictionary or to regress?

Answers to such questions will inevitably reflect the range of different perspectives that represent different individual reading styles; none will be definitively right or wrong. But they will direct the practice read and should, in part, be 'testable' in the process of undertaking the actual practice read. To facilitate this, students should be asked to make a note of every major 'breakpoint' in their reading, and to consider which strategy they used and why; amongst the strategies available will be asking an 'informant', the teacher or a fellow student. The objective is to try to reach an understanding of the text and to learn about the language in parallel.

When the practice read is complete, discussion should focus first on the breakpoints themselves (which were common to most of the group, which to one or two individuals, and why?) and on the strategies used to overcome them. A central element in this discussion will be the evaluation of each strategy (what helped, what didn't and why?) It is the raising of such questions that will lead not only to a continuing dialogue, but also to individual students' monitoring of their own reading.

4.7.3 Search/skim read: evaluating a text: 'Getting the gist', identifying writers' rhetorical purposes

Unlike the listen read and practice read activities above, this activity will not involve an increasingly close and sustained processing of a single text, but an initial skimming of more than one text, followed by scanning for specific items. The extracts selected, ideally two or three contrastive texts, which are either informative or interactive units, or which include both types of unit, should include at least one students are likely to reject and one they may wish, or need, to read in depth. For advanced students, possible genres may be newspapers (for example, controversial editorials, theatre or book reviews, foreign news reports), advertisements or brochures, academic textbooks or papers, manuals (typically evok-ing strong responses). For beginners or less advanced students, genres could include provincial newspapers, which typically contain simple reports of local news, magazines, supermarket promotions, instructions on food products etc.

The basic aims of the activity are first, to encourage students to make efficient use of their time when selecting texts for particular purposes, secondly, to provide them with the opportunity to re-spond affectively to text and to become sensitized to the different rhetorical purposes of the writers of different texts, and thirdly to search for the language items, or 'wordings', and other signals that reveal writer purposes.

With the texts distributed to the students, the activity should start, as indeed all reading lessons should, with an explicit discus-sion of reading purposes and how to achieve them; in this case the focus will be on the need, at times, not only to gain a general impression of a text, but also to do so as quickly and efficiently as possible; hence the real-world need to skim and skip. Students should also be reassured that their personal responses to the texts will be respected.

Attention to such evaluative features of text, in the context of real discourse, is critically important not only as a means of helping second language learners gain entry to the subtleties of English texts, but also as a means of encouraging critical reading in L1.

Directed skimming exercises like this one, encouraging the reader to evaluate different texts instead of merely getting the gist/main point, should also help students to recognize and come to terms with the fact that their response to texts may often be emotional, sometimes with justification and sometimes not. For example, it may be that one of the texts selected is actually required by students for study purposes, yet their initial reaction to the text may be negative. This is not an uncommon experience, but rather one that is inevitable in the course of any academic study. By 'facing' the reality of their own negative responses to a certain text(s), students can take a first step towards considering what strategies for working on the text are most appropriate.

4.7.4   Organizing study reading: scan-reading activities

Like skimming, scanning is a type of reading with which most readers, and certainly EFL learners, will already be familiar. It is also one that probably does not require 'practice', since it is a skill that is a fundamental requirement for survival in any modern community; from our earliest years, we face objects, noticeboards, timetables, headlines, supermarket shelves in order to locate what we need. It is equally obvious that scanning is the most superficial form or part of reading and is not an activity to be pursued as an end in itself. So what place does it have in the classroom?

This depends critically upon the context in which scanning is introduced, the items selected as 'targets' for scanning, how they are selected and where they are searched for. From this it follows that scanning activities should constitute only a part of a more broadly based reading lesson and achieve more broadly based purposes, such as organizing study reading.

For such a purpose, the aim of scanning activities is not to teach students how to scan but to direct their attention to items they will need to attend to, particularly for study purposes. Amongst these, and depending on the profile of our learners, we can include the contents pages of textbooks, the headings and subheadings of academic papers, indices, 'key' words for literature searches, citations, author names, academic departments, publishers and so on. In most contexts, students can and may need to be involved in the selection of targets, particularly in establishing key words for their own areas of study.

Unlike skimming activities that involve students exploring the affective aspects of the interaction between writer and reader, scanning activities are aimed at organizing and structuring the cognitive processing of text. They do this by drawing attention to the guidelines and signals writers provide as a means of entry to the content of a text.

Thus the natural targets for scanning are not features that reflect writer viewpoint etc, but the more formal directions that are an inherent feature of text-books, academic papers, manuals, brochures, reports etc. And the purposes of scanning are not to get a general impression of the text, but to construct a 'map' or 'route' for reflective study reading. From this it follows that the texts selected for scanning activities should be complete, for example a complete chapter, brochure, academic paper. The first step is for students to locate key signals of content in the complete text. The second involves a focus on a single section or chapter and the completion of a graphic outline.

The term graphic outline is widely used in Australian schools participating in a major project, the Effective Use of Reading project which paralleled the British Reading for Learning project. As described by Morris and Stewart-Dore (1984), the graphic outline is designed to ensure that students survey a text in advance of studying it in depth. The outcome is a clear diagram showing what the section being studied is about and how it is organized.

Typically the graphic outline involves the completion of a table or flow diagram with the following headings:

main (or chapter) heading   subheadings   illustrations

With this introduction to scanning activities, we conclude our consideration of 'orienting' reading activities designed to introduce learners to different texts and to find their way into and around them. Such activities are an essential part of any reading programme, particularly programmes designed for students who are grappling with basic decoding, whether of a second or foreign language, or of a highly academic or specialized genre in their mother tongue. But they should not be the core of the reading programme, since the primary goal of reading is understanding and learning.

Thus we turn now to an examination of reading activities that are aimed at achieving these goals. These are reading activities designed to encourage reflective reading.

4.8 Reflective reading

As we saw above, reflective reading involves the reader in an active dialogue with the text; it involves pausing for reflection and it involves in-depth processing of the text.

It is the kind of reading which was promoted by the Schools Council Reading for Learning Project based at Nottingham University from 1978 to 1981. The brief of this project was to work with teachers across the curriculum to develop more effective learning from text. The two major outcomes were the development of a set of active reading tasks designed to encourage reflective reading, which have become known as DARTs, and the identification of a number of different topic-types. As noted in chapter 1, DARTs were designed to offer a radical alternative to traditional comprehension exercises, which were seen to function as 'tests', rather than as learning activities, while the analysis of topic-types and their information constituents, introduced in chapter 3, was intended to provide a principled basis on which to select or design reading activities.

Like most of the activities introduced above, DARTs are applicable at all levels of schooling and across all subject areas, from Infant L1 classrooms to EAP at postgraduate level. Originally trailed and developed by British teachers across the curriculum in secondary and middle schools, they have since been taken up and further developed by teachers in junior and infant schools in Britain, in L2 contexts as varied as ESL, EFL, EAP/ESP, and in Language Across the Curriculum contexts in different parts of the world, for example, Brazil, Singapore, Malaysia, Egypt and New Zealand.

It is DARTs-type activities that are illustrated in this section and summarized in the table on page 154.

From this table it is clear that the range of different DARTs is very wide indeed. It should also be clear that many of the activities included may, at least on the surface, be familiar activities that have been extensively used by teachers in both L1 and L2 contexts in different ways; in their utilization of non-textual forms of representation; for example, tables, diagrams etc, they clearly share features in common with the 'information transfer' activities illustrated by Wallace (1992) and represented in many EFL and EAP course books. At the same time they have much in common with some of the reading activities developed for national testing by the APU team, which were outlined in chapter 1, and also with the 'modelling'or 'non-verbal' strategies developed in the Open University and discussed by Sheldon (1984).

In view of the centrality of reflective reading in any reading programme, and of the range of activities and contexts in which they are used, we need to look at more than one example of reflective reading activities.

4.8.1 A reconstruction activity: word completion

In chapter 1, you undertook a 'word completion' or modified cloze DART. From this you should have seen the potential of such activities for encouraging the motivation to read, for focusing attention on the lexical/semantic relations amongst words in context, for encouraging hypothesis formulation and checking, and in the case of poems etc, for eliciting affective response to text. For the teacher who designed the 'grandmother' cloze which you completed in chapter 1, the objectives of the lesson were (a) to give students the opportunity to understand how a poet achieves certain effects,

DIRECTED ACTIVITIES RELATED TO TEXT

RECONSTRUCTION ACTIVITIES
(using text modified by teacher)

PUPIL TASK: pupils COMPLETE TEXT or diagram, RECONSTRUCTING MEANING.

TEXT COMPLETION
- word completion (selected words deleted from text)
- phrase completion (selected phrases/clauses deleted from text)
- sentence completion (selected sentences deleted from text).

SEQUENCING
- scrambled segments of text arranged in logical/time sequence (text cut into segments representing steps/events etc)
- segments of text classified (texts cut into segments representing certain categories of information).

PREDICTION
- pupils predict next events/step or stage after reading segments of text (text segments presented a section at a time)
- pupils write next part or end of text (text presented a section at a time).

TABLE COMPLETION
- pupils fill in cells of table using row and column headings and text as sources of information (teacher provides row and column headings)
- pupils devise row and column headings using texts and cells of matrix as sources of information (teacher fills in cells).

DIAGRAM COMPLETION
- label completion using text and diagram as sources of information (selected labels deleted from diagrams)
- diagram completion using text and partly complete diagram as sources of information (teacher constructs original diagram: flow diagram, branching tree, network etc).

ANALYSIS ACTIVITIES
(using straight text)

PUPIL TASK: pupils locate and categorize text information by marking and labelling. Use marked text as bases for summary (diagrammatic or note form).

TEXT MARKING
locating and underlining parts of text representing certain meaning of information targets.

LABELLING
pupils label parts of text using labels provided by teacher.

SEGMENTING
pupils break text into meaning or information units and label/annotate segments of text.

TABLE CONSTRUCTION
pupils produce column and row headings for tables and fill in cells using text(s) as source of information.

DIAGRAM CONSTRUCTION
pupils construct and complete diagram appropriate for particular text, for example, FLOW DIAGRAM for text describing a process, BRANCHING TREE for a text describing a hierarchical classification, networks, etc.

PUPIL-GENERATED QUESTIONS
pupils read text and generate questions they still need answers to.

SUMMARY
pupils produce headings and summarize information.

Source: Davies F. and Greene T. 1984

following his or her 'own rules', particularly those governing rhyming pattern and line length, and (b) to help the students to an appreciation of the poem which was in some way their own.

Some impression of the success of the lesson is given in the very short extracts below from the teacher-led plenary session, the full text of which can be found in Lunzer *et al.* (1984). In text **4a**, taken from the introduction to the lesson, the focus is on the rhyming pattern. In text **4b** the focus is on the choice of an appropriate word for the line *too ... (frail) to keep a shop ...* Here it is evident that the constraints on choice are much more subtle, but in a follow-up lesson, the teacher is able to exploit the curiosity aroused by the exercise to explore the tone and mood of the poem in greater depth.

4a

Class discussion

A pupil (unidentified and not always the same): P

Two pupils: PP

Several pupils: Sev

Individuals: S, Ju, Jo, M, Sa

Teacher: T

T   *Now first of all, what have you worked out about the rules? Simon, you arrived at the idea of what rhymes with what quite quickly by yourself. Now – what does rhyme with what?*

S   *After each line, each second line after that rhymes with it and the last two rhyme.*

T   *Yes, and the last two rhyme, the last two rhyme with each other; can you put the other ones a little more plainly?*

S   *The first line rhymes with the third and the second with the fourth.*

T   *Wonderful, yes, in other words alternate lines rhyme. There is a way of describing that when you are talking about poetry which I'll come on to later, but let's leave it out just now. Line 1 rhymes with line 3, line 2 rhymes with line 4, and the last two rhyme. Now that helps you to work out some of the words, particularly in the first verse. What*

about the length of the line? How long are the lines? Did you get anything there?
Ten beats.

4b

'*Later, too frail to keep a shop, she put / All her best things in one long . . .'?*

P   *'Empty'.*

P   *'Lovely,' 'dark.'*

T   *'. . . in one long empty room', '. . . lovely room'?*

P   *Don't like 'lovely'.*

T   *You don't like 'lovely'.*

Sev   *No.*

P   *She would lock her antiques in a lovely room, wouldn't she?*

P   *Yes, just as well as in your dark rooms . . . if she was saving them.*

T   *What, in a lovely room?*

P   *Yes.*

P   *But she's storing them away, too frail to carry on with the shop, so she's picking out the best to store away. She wouldn't put them in a beautiful room, would she?*

(From Lunzer *et al.*)

4.8.2   A multiple DART: text marking, diagram completion and table completion

In a further example of a research-oriented activity, you were also introduced, in chapter 1, to a table completion task that involved a group of students studying a text on Tooth Structure and completing a table with column headings shown below:

part   location   property   function

This table completion activity had, however, been preceded by two other tasks, first, a text-marking activity involving students in locating and underlining all the <u>parts of the tooth</u>. This was followed by a diagram completion task in which certain labels had been deleted from the diagram of the tooth; the student task was to read the text and study the remaining labels in the text in order to complete the labelling. Such diagram completion tasks are seen by teachers to be an essential first step for learning from topic-types such as physical structure and mechanism. It should also be noted that this multiple DART, like all such reading activities, was based upon a prior analysis of the textual unit, in this case through reference to the information constituents of the topic-type; physical structure.

4.8.3   The wide-ranging potential of text marking and table completion

However, while we can see that diagram completion is an activity restricted to texts/extracts in which a diagram accompanies the text, the potential of text marking and table completion are not so restricted. Indeed, of all the reflective reading activities, these appear to have the most extensive application for a very wide range of texts and contexts.

Text marking

Unlike word and diagram completion, in text marking there does not appear to be anything missing. The text or extract is not modified or cut up, but presented complete. The function of text marking is that it permits the student to 'pin down' and highlight key elements in the text, typically the 'targets' set by the teacher. As we have seen, in a physical structure text these may be the parts of the structure; but equally in a novel, they may be the parts of the text that express the feelings of a particular character, or the aspects of the setting that contribute to the force of the narrative; in an EFL text, the target may be the verbs that express 'states' or the 'words or phrases that link paragraphs'. It is such language/ functional items that you were asked to search for when you analysed the extracts from the Undergraduate Prospectus in chapter 3. My prediction is that you did, or were certainly tempted, to mark the text. Hence the wide-ranging potential of text marking.

Table completion

By contrast with text marking, table completion does not pin down, but rather provides a framework within which to classify the information in the text: the schematic framework hidden behind the text. It is this that, at least initially, is provided by the teacher through preparing the headings for columns and rows that learners use to direct their reading of text. However, the long-term objective is that the framework is gradually internalized by students as a basis for their own independent study; in the short run, of course, the completed table provides a framework and database for writing or summarizing information. As such it obviates the need for the strategy of 'copying', which, as we saw in chapter 1, Nicholson reported as the dominant strategy in the junior high school.

The methodology is as appropriate for beginning readers, as for junior, EFL and secondary students. For instance, a group of beginners can be led by their teacher through a reading of a descriptive text such as those produced in New Zealand by Ashton Scholastic, from which the extract below is taken. In this *What Do You Do*? series, 'friendly' creatures such as Dilly Duck, Freddie Fish etc, are introduced through pictures and text that tell us what each creature says, where he/she lives, and what each does. These are the column labels, the creatures providing the labels for the rows.

4d

What do you do Freddie Fish, Freddie Fish?
What do you do Freddie Fish?

I wriggle and swim
and dive through the foam
I play in the seaweed
and hide all alone
from big fish who chase me.
Then off I go home.

From Blackburn and Handy (1975)

4.8.4 From table completion to labelling and table construction

In higher education, postgraduate students in EAP make use of
table completion as a technique for analysing and summarizing the
information from longer stretches of text, or for summarizing and
comparing the perspectives and findings of several texts or academic papers. At this level, the exercise becomes a table construction task rather than a table completion task. As such, it inevitably
involves as a first step, the reading or search reading of the text in
order to label the key topics, perspectives etc that will become the
headings for the table. We will return to the activity of labelling
below.

ACTIVITY

If you yourself are currently studying for a diploma or master's
degree you should test the potential of this procedure or strategy
through your own reading, selecting at least two 'texts', for example, books or academic papers on the same topic. Your first task
will be to do a preliminary search read in order to identify the

criteria for comparison. These will provide you with at least preliminary headings for your table. For instance, if you choose to compare different views of the teaching of reading, the initial headings you identify may be: model of reading used, definition or description of text, strategies recommended etc.

4.8.5 Prediction activities

In chapter 2 we saw the potential of Rumelhart's on-line prediction procedure as a means of investigating the process of reading. Here we explore prediction as an activity that has rich potential at all levels of reading development and in all contexts.

Here we will take, as a first example, a prediction activity in an infant classroom. For this activity, with a group of beginning readers, the teacher selects a familiar story which is presented so that it can be read by all in the group, for instance on a flip chart, in the form of a 'giant' book, and/or in copies of the text for each child.

The first objective is to give children experience of predicting and following the structure of the story, using their previous knowledge of the characters and their goals. So the teacher elicits from the children, for instance, the title of the story, the names of the characters and the setting of the story. Each response is discussed and evaluated in turn and when agreed to be 'correct' or 'true', is identified in the text.

The next stage involves predicting what 'happens' in the story: again predictions are evaluated and then checked out against the text. Checking out involves reference to previous knowledge, to 'sense', to known words, to analogous words, to word endings or beginnings, to regular correspondences between letters and sounds and perhaps also to grammatical knowledge and/or pictures.

A simple, indeed quite traditional lesson; however, it serves to illustrate two key features of active reading lessons; first, the fact that they involve overt hypothesis generation and testing of the kind embodied in Rumelhart's model of reading, and secondly, the checking of these predictions against a range of sources of information, including other readers. Thus in this emphasis on the checking and revision of hypotheses, prediction activities are sharply contrasted with the kinds of prediction exercises that encourage students to <u>rely</u> on predictions and to be satisfied with the 'gist' of a text.

These are also features of prediction activities that are followed in other contexts, for example, in the junior L1 or EFL classroom, students are presented with a segment of text that introduces a new, rather than an unknown story. In this the main setting of the story is established and the main characters and their goals are introduced. The task here is for students working in twos and threes to predict the final resolution of the story.

Provided that characters' goals are clear in the first segment of text, students are frequently very close to the original in their predictions, though variations are naturally welcomed and typically defended by their 'authors'.

This suggests that readers not only utilize their knowledge of the narrative schema, which we were introduced to in chapter 3, to guide their processing of the text, but that they are sensitive to the linguistic forms that realize elements of the story such as setting, goals, attempts, outcomes, resolution.

Once predictions have been made, students are then asked to find the parts of the text that gave them the most clues about how the story would end. In doing so they have a chance to explore in depth the relation between language choice and meaning. Subsequent stages of such a prediction activity include the prediction of the episodes that lead to the final resolution and the checking of these against further segments of text, the study of character through looking at the parts of the text that provide information about characters' qualities and/or the construction of alternative versions.

However, prediction activities are not restricted to the infant or junior classroom or to narrative; teachers of language and literature at higher levels of schooling make extensive use of prediction to examine key sections of longer text, with predictions sometimes going forward in the text and sometimes looking back. Teachers working in EFL and EAP make use of prediction as a means of entry to interactive texts or units of texts, for example, introductions and discussion sections of academic articles and editorials.

Up to this point, then, the activities we have examined are activities that in one form or another were introduced in earlier chapters. We need now to seek to extend our repertoire of activities for encouraging reflective reading.

4.8.6 Segmenting and sequencing

The potential of segmenting and sequencing is also widely exploited in a range of different contexts, particularly with texts describing processes of different kinds. Text **4d** below was first used with a class of ten-year-olds working in twos or threes, who were asked to mark the texts with a slash (/) at every step or stage of the process, and then to number the steps or stages. Some students in the class marked as many as seventeen 'steps', others as few as seven 'stages'. Class discussion focused initially on the (useful) ambiguity of the instruction; is there any difference between a step and a stage and how do steps constitute stages?

4d

PULP MILL

At the pulp mill the logs first go into the barking plant. Here any remaining bark is stripped off the wood and the pieces of bark are washed away by water. The wood is then chipped up by machines and the wood chips are cooked with chemicals in large tanks known as digesters, of which Mantta has 6. This reduces the wood chips to wood pulp, which consists largely of cellulose.

In the paper mill the pulp is boiled with more chemicals and bleached, the bleach being removed by further washing with fresh water. Next, the cellulose fibres in the pulp are separated out by a process known as beating, which is carried out in large tanks, and the result looks like rather thick cream. This 'cream' is thinned by adding water, and the liquid which consists now of about 99 parts water and 1 part cellulose, is fed by machine on to a moving belt or apron made of very fine-meshed wire. The machine is designed to spread an even layer over the apron which may be as much as 10 or 12 feet wide. As the apron moves on an even sheet of something looking like thick, wet paper begins to form. Much of the water drips through the wire mesh, and more is removed by suction as the apron passes over suction boxes, but the paper still contains a large amount of moisture and further steps are taken to dry it. It leaves the wire apron and is fed on to a large conveyor belt made of felt. This carries the paper slowly through sets of rollers. Some of these just squeeze the water out; others are gently heated to help with the drying. When this process is complete the paper is reeled off on to large wooden bobbins.

(Rushby *et al.* 1975)

4.8.7 Labelling revisited

From here the focus of the lesson was on the important problem of labelling, rather than numbering, the different stages. A further issue considered was the difference between simultaneous actions and sequential actions. As always in a DART lesson, careful reference had to be made to the text to resolve this. What is of particular interest here, however, is that this text, and variations of the DART, have subsequently been used in quite different contexts from the original, first with groups of EAP postgraduate engineers, and secondly with groups of teachers from extremely varied language, cultural and institutional backgrounds.

In all groups the initial range of responses is similar to that of the original class of lower secondary students and in all groups the issues raised in discussion have been similar, although these have naturally been extended in the teacher groups. What have varied, however, have been the terms used for labelling. In the original group these were '-ing' nouns formed from words in the text and included labels like: 'barking', 'stripping', 'chipping', 'pulping', 'bleaching', 'spreading', 'dripping', 'drying', 'suction'. With more sophisticated groups, the noun form may include '-ion' and more abstract nouns are also suggested: 'preparation', 'processing', 'refining', 'extraction', 'finishing', 'drying', 'forming'.

For all teachers this type of task illustrates the potential of labelling as a means of abstracting and organizing knowledge; for language teachers it suggests the need to pay much greater attention to lexis and to the cohesive relations between words. It also illustrates the potential of such activities to lead into a very explicit study of vocabulary in context. In this text, the labelling task represents one route to vocabulary study.

4.8.8 Text marking as an entry to cohesion

An alternative or additional task is to mark in the text all the references to the material or object being transformed. This typically results in a list like the following: *logs, wood, wood chips, wood pulp (cellulose), pulp, cellulose fibres in the pulp, cream, an even layer, paper* etc. As I have noted previously (Davies 1986b), what is striking about this list is that it 'refers to' a single 'entity' the essential wood/pulp/paper. However, the relation between the words that refer to the entity is not exactly one of equivalence since the form of the entity changes at each stage of the process. The lexico-semantic relation that it represents, then, is one of transformation and is one that you may seek to identify in other descriptions of processes.

Of further interest, particularly to language teachers, is the way in which this text illustrates the potential of topic-type analysis. The reading activities above showed that there are a number of points of entry to any text. In the case of this text, which is a process topic-type, it is the information constituents that suggest alternative points of entry: the material or object being transformed, the stages of the process, the action, the instrument or agent of transformation.

4.9 Selecting tasks for different texts and textual units

With the above examples the potential and 'fun' of active reading tasks have been illustrated, and it should also be clear that they represent a radical alternative to the typical reading lesson with its tidy question-and-answer format and right and wrong answers.

The question that remains is: what activities to select for what purpose(s) and what text? In practice, of course, the question is one that can only be answered by the classroom teacher with his or her knowledge of specific groups of students. However, it is possible to take a first step towards answering this question through reference to the rule-of-thumb 'guide' presented in the table on page 166.

From the above it could appear that the guide provides a simple route to the selection of a reading activity. For this reason caution is needed, and it should be noted that the relationship between reading activity and text-type is only a general one and does not represent a one-to-one correspondence. Thus it is suggested that teachers use the table as a rather simplistic guide in the initial stages of designing DARTs, but that they seek to challenge it as they gain more confidence of what works with the specific tasks in their programme and their specific groups of learners. It should

For Narrative Argument texts	text marking
	prediction
	sequencing
	segmenting
	labelling
	completion activities, for example,
	phrase/sentence
For Physical Structure and Mechanism Topic-Types	text marking
	diagram labelling and completion*
	table completion
For Social Structure, State–Situation and Classification Topic-Types	text marking
	hierarchy/branching tree
	diagrams and flow chart
	labelling
	table completion
For process Topic-Type	text marking
	flow diagram
	segmenting
	labelling
	table completion
Instruction Topic-Type	sequencing
For Theory/Force Topic-Types	text marking
	labelling
	table completion

also be noted that there are a number of topic-types in the table which, for reasons of space, are not dealt with in this chapter.

SUMMARY

- Every learner brings to the reading classroom an individual set of purposes, perceptions, preferences, personal responses and a set of strategies for approaching reading tasks.

Designing a reading programme and reading activities

- The design of a reading programme should be based on a systematic analysis of the needs, perceptions and background of the specific group of students being taught and not on generalized prescriptions about reading.
- In investigating such factors, teachers can draw upon a range of methods, many of which are utilized in the reasearch studies described in chapter 1.
- In designing reading programmes teachers also need to develop their own criteria for selecting texts for specific groups of students.
- A consideration of different reading purposes and different types of reading by both teachers and students should be a central element in the teaching of reading.
- The reading programme should provide opportunities for students to engage in different types of reading for different purposes and to evaluate them in discussion with their peers and teachers.
- The reading tasks used in the classroom should be activities which encourage active engagement with and analysis of texts rather than be passive 'testing' exercises.
- In designing reading activities teachers will find it helpful to take account of the distinctive structure and linguisitic features of the genres/texts selected for study.

Glossary

active reading tasks Reading activities or tasks that involve readers in an interactive 'dialogue' with the text, and hence in critical directed analysis of a text or in the reconstruction of a text that is incomplete in some way. (see also **DARTs**).

affective factors in reading Factors relating to readers' attitudes to reading, their motivation to read different texts in different contexts, and their emotional response to reading different texts.

anchor A term introduced by Hedge (1991) to refer to the knowledge-based sources of information drawn upon selectively in the process of reading.

authentic or real texts Texts selected by a reader or a teacher which are recognized by the reader as meeting some need for information, entertainment, aesthetic satisfaction or instruction and which provide a meaningful context for learning aspects and patterns of language.

bottom-up models of reading Models of the reading process that describe the process as a sequence of discrete 'steps' in which the direction of processing is from 'bottom-level' features of text to 'higher levels', that is, from the identification of letters to sounds, to words, to sentences and finally to meaning and thinking.

cloze procedure As developed by Taylor (1953), a technique for measuring the relative 'readability' of a text by asking readers to fill in the gaps left by deleting every nth word, for example, every fifth word. Modified forms of cloze do not involve the deletion of every nth word, but the selective deletion of words or phrases which will create a text-based problem-solving exercise.

coherence   The extent to which a text or discourse is perceived to function as a meaningful whole.

cohesion   The grammatical and lexical items that provide 'ties' or links across sentences in text.

control strategies   see **types of strategy** below.

DARTs, or **Directed Activities Related to Text**   The set of active reading tasks developed by the Reading for Learning team (see Lunzer *et al.* 1984 and Davies and Greene 1984) and classified as either <u>analytic</u> activities, for example, text marking, diagram construction segmenting etc or <u>reconstruction</u> activities, for example, modified cloze, sequencing.

decode   The process of matching written forms of the language with spoken forms.

discourse type   In this volume the term given to descriptions of text through reference to the general rhetorical goals, for example, description, exposition, persuasion, literary-poetic, didactic.

drivers   The term coined by Hedge (1991) to refer to different types of reading purpose.

eye fixation   The physical stage of the reading process when the eyes are not moving but are fixed on a stretch of print; it is during a fixation that the information from the printed text is actually analysed and processed by the eye and the brain. From their experimental data, Rayner and Pollatsek observe that the fixation is limited to a (universal) 'perceptual span', which extends only to about fifteen characters. The fixation typically lasts for about 250 msecs.

fovea   The part of the eye which functions as the focusing mechanism during a fixation.

genre   In this volume two definitions of genre are presented:
— genre as process: the staged goal-oriented social processes underlying a class of texts;
— genre as object: a class of (written) texts that reflect a particular set of social processes and goals and derive from an identifiable and public

source/environment, and are directly or indirectly controlled by an 'editor'.

grapho-phonic rules The rules that describe the correspondences between the letters and spelling patterns of a language and their phonological, or sound, equivalents.

higher-order reading skills A term used loosely to refer to the processes activated in reading for meaning and critical reading, for example, predicting outcomes, reflecting, questioning the text.

hypothesis In the context of reading, a hypothesis is a more or less well-informed prediction about the identity or meaning of a word or group of words in a text.

hypothesis generation and testing The process, during reading, of making informed guesses about word or meaning identification and of checking the validity of the guesses.

interaction with text/other readers The cognitive and affective processes of reflecting upon a statement in a text, questioning the text or responding emotionally to the text, and/or the social activity of sharing this response with other readers. (See also **types of strategy**.)

interactive models of reading Models of reading which predict that the different sources of information available in the reading process interact with each other, either supporting or refuting readers' initial hypotheses. In such models, the reader is seen to be able to draw simultaneously, but selectively, upon a range of sources of information: visual, orthographic, lexical, semantic, syntactic and schematic, and they incorporate the mechanism of parallel processing, that is, the simultaneous processing of information from more than one source. Hence interactive models do not predict any preferred sequence of processing.

introspective data and methods Methods for investigating reading behaviour which involve the collection and anaylsis of readers' reports (or protocols) of what they are thinking, feeling or doing during the process of reading. Different types of introspective data include:
— **think-aloud** data collected from individual readers who report on what they are thinking during the process of reading;

—**talk-aloud** data collected from pairs or groups of readers as they discuss their views during a reading task;

—**retrospection** data collected from readers who report on their thinking after the reading task is completed.

—**lexico-semantic relations** meaning relations which hold between or amongst words or groups of words (lexical items) which reveal their similarities, e.g. equivalence, or differences e.g. opposition.

miscue analysis   The analysis of oral reading errors, as a means of understanding the 'cues' or sources of information that gave rise to the error.

modes of reading   A classification by Hedge (1991) of six different types of reading behaviour through reference to the route used to comprehend a text, for example, from bottom-up to interactive, or from top-down to interactive. As an alternative to abstract models of reading, modes represent a taxonomy of reading behaviour which can be used to study individual readers.

monitor the reading process   see **types of strategy**.

mode   One of a sequence of communicative actions or interactive units selected by an author as a means of presenting his or her message to the reader. (See also **textual units** and **structure**.)

narrative structure   The sequence of interactive units or elements that constitute the typical narrative; for example, setting or orientation, complicating action, evaluation and resolution. (See also **structure**.)

parallel processing   see **interactive models of reading**

passive reading tasks   Reading activities that do not require the reader to engage analytically or critically with a text, for example, comprehension 'exercises'.

perceptual span   The stretch of print that can be physically and cognitively attended to and processed during the fixation of the eyes. (See also **eye fixation**.)

problem–solution pattern   A rhetorical or communicative pattern used for the presentation of information about real-world problems and frequently found in popular science journals and engineering reports; typical elements are situation, problem, response, evaluation and basis for evaluation. (See also **structure**.)

protocols   The records, either on tape or in the form of a transcription, of subjects' reports of their thinking processes. See also **introspective methods**.

real texts   see **authentic or real texts**.

readability   A measure of the predicted difficulty of a text through reference to readability formulae of different kinds.

register   As used by linguists following Halliday (1985, 1988 and 1985/89) the term register refers to aspects of the context of situation of a text and includes the **field**, the social processes taking place, **tenor**, the role relationship between participants and **mode**, the organization and 'style' of the message.

regression   The movement of the eyes to fixate on a previous part of the text.

reliability   The extent to which a test produces consistent results when administered under similar conditions.

rhetorical pattern   A communicative device for signalling the logical or rhetorical relationships amongst clauses in a text; for example, contrast, similarity, general statement-specific example, problem–solution.

schema   A unit of knowledge that is part of the total set of schemata individuals are constantly recreating and upon which they draw in interpreting the world. With respect to reading it is assumed that readers need to activate apropriate schemata for each new text they encounter; schematic knowledge is also referred to as background knowledge and includes knowledge about content, culture, text structure, rhetorical patterns etc and also information about how the knowledge is to be used.

self-correction   The process of correcting an error, or miscue, in reading aloud.

simplified texts   see **structured reading schemes**.

strategy   A physical or mental action used consciously or unconsciously for the purpose of facilitating text comprehension and/or learning. (See also **types of strategy**.)

structure of text   The rhetorical or communicative patterns that result from the selection of certain communicative or functional elements in different texts, for example, narrative structure, problem–solution structure etc.

structured reading schemes or **simplified texts**   Texts selected by a textbook writer or teacher for the purpose of teaching a preselected item or aspect of language: for example, phonic rules, the shape of a word, a linguistic structure, where context is strictly controlled in order to focus attention on the feature of language targeted.

substitution   One of the most common errors, or miscues, in reading, wherein a word or phrase in the text is substituted by a word not in the text. (See **miscue analysis**.)

text   A coherent piece of writing, exhibiting both **structure** and **texture**, assignable to a single author or collaborating authors, with clearly defined boundaries marking the beginning and the end of the writing.

textual unit   A part of a complete text that serves a specific communicative function within the text which is reflected in the position it occupies within the text; in this volume three distinct types of texual unit are proposed:
— interactive text-types, predominantly, though not exclusively, concerned with negotiating the relationship between writer and reader and hence expressing the interpersonal function of language;
— organizational text-types, or linkers, predominantly though not exclusively concerned with linking one part of the text with another and hence with expressing the textual function of language;
— topical or informing text-types, predominantly though not exclusively concerned with presenting information, and hence expressing the logical/experimental or ideational function of language.

texture   see **text**.

theme   The first grammatical constituent of a clause or sentence; that is grammatical Subject, Adjunct, Complement or Predicator; in declarative sentences, the typical, or unmarked choice of Subject. Theme analysis is concerned with analysing the patterns of theme choice over units or over whole texts and with establishing the communicative function of such patterns of choice.

top-down models of reading Models of the reading process which predict that the processing sequence proceeds from predictions about meaning to attention to progressively smaller units, for example, letters, visual features.

topic-type A classification of different topical or informing units of text through reference to their information constituents, for example, a description of the topic-type physical structure is made up of the information constituents: parts, properties, location and function.

types of reading Reading behaviours classified through reference to the relative pace and focus of attention during the reading; in this volume, five distinct types of reading are identified:
— LISTEN READ as a route to either RECEPTIVE or REFLECTIVE READING for the purposes of pleasure and learning about text structure and the relation between print and speech;
— PRACTICE READ, involving slow, hesitant text processing aimed at understanding of context but also requiring conscious attention to lower-level orthographic or lexical or syntactic features of text, for the dual pupodes of understanding in depth and learning about the language system;
— SEARCH READ (a)/skim of the text for the purposes of 'getting the gist' and/or as a route to critical evaluation of texts;
— SEARCH READ (b)/scan to locate specific items of information for the purposes of organizing study reading;
— REFLECTIVE READING, involving in-depth reading, pausing, regression and reflection on what is read for purposes of learning and appreciation;
— RECEPTIVE READING, involving a smooth, typically unconscious reading of undemanding, familiar or narrative text, for pleasure and 'unconscious' language learning.

types of strategy In this volume, five broad types of reading strategy are proposed:

— control reading process by engaging consciously or unconsciously in action that is observable, for example, regressing, pausing, marking text;

— monitor reading process, by consciously attempting to find ways into the meaning of the text and/or by evaluating such attempts;

— interact with text, by questioning, expressing feelings etc on the basis of at least an interim interpretation of the text; hence interaction represents a response to text rather than the evaluation of a route into the text;

— utilize source of information: textual, by paying attention to linguistic features of the text, and/or one's textual/linguistic knowledge as it is evoked by reading the text, for example, grammar, repetition of words, text structure etc;

— utilize source of information: external/background knowledge, by drawing on non-textual knowledge which may be evoked by, but is not given in the text, for example, knowledge of topic, content area, culture etc.

validity The extent to which a test procedure serves the uses for which it was intended.

utilize source of information   see **types of strategy**.

word class   The classification of words that is defined through reference to their function in the grammatical structure of a group (or phrase), for example, noun, verb, adjective etc.

References

Alderson J. 1979a. The cloze procedure and proficiency in English. *TESOL Quarterly*, 13, 219–28.

Alderson J. 1979b. The effect on the cloze test of changes in deletion frequency. *TESOL Quarterly*, 13, 219–27.

Alderson J. 1980. Native and non-native speaker performance on cloze tests. *Language Learning*, 30, 59–76.

Alderson, J. and A. Urquhart. 1984. *Reading in a Foreign Language*. New York: Longman.

Barnett, M. A. 1989. *More than Meets the Eye: Foreign Language Reading, Theory and Practice*. Englewood Cliffs, NJ: Prentice Hall.

Bensoussan, M. 1990. Redundancy and cohesive cloze. *Research in Reading*, 13, 1, 18–37.

Bernhardt, E. B. 1991. *Reading Development in a Second Language: Theoretical, Empirical and Classroom Perspectives*. Norwood, NJ: Ablex Publishing.

Bloom, B. *et al.* 1965. *Taxonomy of Educational Objectives 1: Cognitive Domain*. New York: David McKay.

Brewer, W. F. 1980. Literary theory, rhetoric and stylistics: implications for psychology. In R. J. Spiro, B. C. Bruce and W. F. Brewer (eds.) *Theoretical Issues in reading Comprehension: Perspectives from Cognitive Psychology, Linguistics, Artificial Intelligence and Education*. Hillsdale. NJ: Lawrence Erlbaum.

Carrell, P. L. 1983b. Some issues in studying the role of schemata, or background knowledge, in second language comprehension. *Reading in a Foreign Language*, 1, 2, 81–92.

Carrell, P. L. 1984. Evidence of a formal schema in second language comprehension. *Language Learning*, 34, 2, 87–112.

Carrell, P. L. 1987. Content and formal schemata in ESL reading. *TESOL Quarterly*, 21, 3, 461–81.

Carrell, P. L., J. Devine and **D. E. Eskey** (eds.) 1988. *Interactive Approaches to Second Language Reading*, Cambridge: Cambridge University Press.

Carter, R. (ed.). 1990. *Knowledge About Language and the Curriculum: The LINC Reader*. Sevenoaks: Hodder and Stoughton.

Carter, R. ms. *Language in the National Curriculum: Materials for Professional Development.* Nottingham: University of Nottingham Press.

Clay, M. M. 1968. A syntactic analysis of reading errors. *Journal of Verbal Learning and Verbal Behaviour*, 7, 434–8.

Clay, M. M. 1969. Reading errors and self-correction behaviour. *British Journal of Psychology*, 39, 47–56.

Clay, M. M. 1979/92. *The Early Detection of Reading Difficulties.* Newcastle-upon-Tyne: Heinemann.

Cohen, A. D. 1986. Mentalistic measures in reading strategy research: some recent findings. *English for Specific Purposes*, 5, 2, 131–45.

Cortazzi, M. 1993. *Narrative Analysis*. London: The Falmer Press.

Couture, B. (ed.). 1986. *Functional Approaches to Writing: Research Perspectives*. London: Frances Pinter.

Davies, F. and **T. Greene.** 1982. Directed activities related to text: text analysis and text reconstruction. *ERIC Clearing House on Communication Skills and Reading, Abstract in Resources in Education*, March 1982.

Davies, F. and **T. Greene.** 1984. *Reading for Learning in the Sciences.* Edinburgh: Oliver and Boyd.

Davies, F. 1985. Towards a classroom based methodology for identifying information structures in texts in specific subject areas. In J. M. Ulijn and A. K. Pugh (eds.) 1985 *Reading for Professional Purposes: Methods and Materials in Teaching Languages.* Leuven, Belgium, ACCO Contrastive Analysis Series.

Davies, F. 1986a. *Books in the School Curriculum: A Compilation and Review of Research Relating to Voluntary and Intensive Reading.* London: The Publishers' Association for The National Book League.

Davies, F. 1986b. The structure and language of textbooks across the curriculum. In M. Tickoo (ed.) *Language in Learning.* Singapore: RELC Anthology Series 16.

Davies, F. 1988. Designing a writing syllabus in English for academic purposes: process and product. In P. Robinson (ed.) *Academic Writing: Process and Product.* New York: Macmillan MEP.

References

Davies, F. 1990. Reading in the national curriculum: implications for primary and secondary classrooms. In J. Harris and J. Wilkinson (eds.) *In the Know: A Guide to English and the National Curriculum*, Cheltenham: Stanley Thornes.

Davies, F. 1993. The language of textbooks. In R. E. Asher (ed.) *The Encyclopedia of Language and Linguistics*, 9. Oxford: Pergamon Press.

Davies F. 1994a (forthcoming). Marked theme as a heuristic for analysing text-type, text and genre. In J. Pique and D. J. Viera (ed.) *Applied Languages: Theory and Practice in ESP*. Valencia: Universidad de Valencia.

Davies, F. 1994b (forthcoming). From writer roles to elements of text. In L. Barbara and M. Scott (eds.) *Reflections on Language Learning*. Clevedon, UK: Multilingual Matters.

Devine, J., P. L. Carrell and D. E. Eskey (eds.) 1987. Research in reading in English as a second language. Washington DC: TESOL.

Durkin, D. 1978. What classroom observations reveal about reading comprehension instruction. *Reading Research Quarterly*, 14, 4, 481–533.

Eskey, D. 1988. Holding in at the bottom: an interactive approach to the language problems of second language readers. In Carrell, Devine and Eskey, op. cit.

Exton, G. and P. O'Rourke. 'KAL' and Real books/reading schemes. *Reading*, 27, 2, July 1993, and 27–9.

Faerch, C. and Kasper, G. (eds.). 1987. *Introspection in Second Language Research*. Clevedon, UK: Multilingual Matters.

Goodman, K. S. 1969. Analysis of oral reading miscues: applied psycholinguistics. *Reading Research Quarterly*, 5, 9–30.

Goodman, K. S. 1970. Reading: a psycholinguistic guessing game. In H. Singer and R. B. Ruddell, (eds.) *Theoretical Models and Processes of Reading*. Newark, Delaware: International Reading Association.

Goodman, K. S. 1975. The reading process. In F. W. Gollasch, 1975 reprinted in Carrell, Devine and Eskey op. cit.

Goodman, K. S. 1988. The reading process. In Carrell, Devine and Eskey op. cit.

Gorman, T., J. White, L. Orchard and A.Tate 1981. *Language Performance in Schools, Primary Reports 1 and 2*. London: HMSO (Assessment of Performance Unit).

Gorman, T., J. White, L. Orchard and A. Tate 1982. *Language Perform-*

ance in Schools: Secondary Survey Reports 1 and 2. London: HMSO (Assessment of Performance Unit).

Gough, P. B. 1972. One second of reading. In Kavanagh and Mattingly (eds.) 1972. *Language by Ear and by Eye.* Cambridge, Mass.: MIT Press.

Haarstrup, K. 1987. Using think-aloud and retrospection to uncover learner's lexical inferencing procedures. In Faerch and Kasper op. cit.

Halliday, M. A. K. and **R. Hasan.** 1976. *Cohesion in English.* London: Longman.

Halliday, M. A. K. 1985. *An Introduction to Functional Grammar.* London: Edward Arnold.

Halliday, M. A. K. and **R. Hasan.** 1985/89. *Language, Text and Context: Aspects of Language in a Social/Semiotic Perspective.* Oxford: Oxford University Press.

Halliday, M. A. K. 1989. *Spoken and Written Language.* London: Oxford University Press.

Harri-Augstein, S. and **L. Thomas.** 1984. Conversational investigations of reading: the self-organised learner and the text. In Alderson and Urquhart, op. cit.

Harrison, C. 1980. *Readability in the classroom.* Cambridge: University of Cambridge Press Syndicate.

Heather, P. 1981. Young people's reading: A study of the leisure reading of 13–15-year-olds. Occasional Paper 6, London British Library Board.

Hedge, N. 1991. Reading and learning: an exploration of perception, approaches and strategies of overseas postgraduates using English for academic purposes. Unpublished Ph.D. thesis. University of Liverpool.

Hedge, N. and **H. Gosden.** 1991. Language Awareness and EAP Courses. In C. James and P. Garrett *Language Awareness in the Classroom.* Harlow: Longman.

Hoey, M. 1983a/91. *On the Surface of Discourse.* London/Nottingham: Allen and Unwin/Nottingham University.

Hosenfeld, C. 1977b. A preliminary investigation of the reading strategies of successful and unsuccessful second language learners. *System*, 5, 110–23.

Hosenfeld, C., V. Arnold, J. Kirchofer, J. Laciura and **L. Wilson.** 1981. Second language reading: a curricular sequence for teaching reading strategies. *Foreign Language Annals*, 14, 5, 415–422.

References

Hosenfeld, C. 1984. Case studies of ninth-grade readers. In Alderson and Urquhart (eds.) op. cit.

Ingham, J. 1981. *Books and Reading Development: The Bradford Book Flood.* London: Heinemann.

Johns, A. 1988. Reading for summarizing: an approach to text orientation and processing, *Reading in a Foreign Language*, 4, 2.

Johns, T. and F. Davies. Text as a vehicle for information: the classroom use of written texts in teaching reading in a foreign language, *Reading in a Foreign Language*, 1, 1, 1–19.

Jonz, J. 1990. Another turn in the conversation: what does cloze measure? *TESOL Quarterly*, 24, 1, 61–83.

Kletzien, S. B. 1991. Strategy use by good and poor comprehenders reading expository text of differing levels. *Reading Research Quarterly*, 26, 1, 67–85.

Labov, W. 1972. The transformation of experience in narrative syntax. In W. Labov. *Language of the Inner City*. Oxford: Basil Blackwell.

LINC (Language in the National Curriculum) Project Materials 1992. Obtainable from Department of English Studies, University of Nottingham.

Lunzer, E. and K. Gardner (eds.). 1979. *The Effective Use of Reading*. London: Heinemann.

Lunzer, E., K. Gardner, F. Davies and T. Greene. (1984). *Learning from the Written Word*. Edinburgh: Oliver and Boyd.

McClelland, J. L., D. E. Rumelhart and the PDP Research Group. 1986/1989. *Parallel Distributed Processing: Explorations in the Microstructure of Cognition, Volume 2: Psychological and Biological Models.* Cambridge, Mass.: MIT Press.

McLeod, J. 1970. *Manual: Gap Reading Comprehension Test*. London: Heinemann.

McLeod, J. and J. Anderson. 1973. Manual: Gapadol Reading Comprehension Test. London: Heinemann.

Martin, J. R. 1984. Language register and genre. In F. Christie *et al.* (eds.) *Children Writing: Reader ECT418 Language Studies*. Victoria: Victoria University Press.

Martin, J. 1992. *English Text: System and Structure.* Philadelphia/Amsterdam: John Benjamin.

Mason, M. 1992. Illuminating English: how explicit language teaching improved public examination results in a comprehensive school, *Educational Studies*, 18, 3, 341–353.

Mathewson, G. 1985. Towards a comprehensive model of affect in the reading process. In H. Singer and R. B. Ruddell. *Theoretical Models and Processes of Reading*. Newark, Delaware: International Reading Association.

Meek, M. 1988. *How Texts Teach What Readers Have to Learn*. Stroud: Thimble Press.

Meek, M. 1990. What do we know about reading that helps us teach? In Carter R. (ed.) 199, op. cit.

Meyer, B. 1992. An analysis of a plea for money. In W. C. Mann and S. A. Thompson (1992), *Diverse Linguistic Analyses of a Fund-Raising Text* Philadelphia/Amsterdam: John Benjamin.

Meyer, B. and **R. Freedle.** 1975. The effects of different prose types on recall. *American Educational Research Journal* 21, 1, 121–43.

Meyer, B. and **G. E. Rice.** 1982. The interaction of reader strategies and the organization of text. *Text* 2, 1, 155–92.

Morris, A. and **N. Stewart-Dore.** 1984. *Learning to Learn from Text: Effective Reading in the Content Areas*. North Ryde, NSW.: Addison-Wesley.

Neale, M. 1958. *Analysis of Reading Ability*. London: Macmillan.

Nicholson, T. 1982. *A Study of Reading and Learning in the Junior Secondary School: Final Report of the Project*. Waikato, N.Z.: University of Waikato.

Nicholson, T. 1984. Experts and novices: a study of reading in the high school classroom. *Reading Research Quarterly*, 19, 4, 436–51.

Nicholson, T. 1985. The confusing world of high school reading. *Journal of Reading*, 28, 6, 514–27.

Oh, J. 1990. On the relationship between anxiety and reading in English as a foreign language among Korean university students in Korea. Unpublished Ph.D. Dissertation. University of Texas.

Perera, K. 1984. *Children's Writing and Recording*. Oxford: Basil Blackwell.

Pritchard, R. 1990. The effects of cultural schemata on reading processing strategies. *Reading Research Quarterly*, 25, 4, 273–91.

Rayner, K. and **A. Pollatsek.** 1989. *The Psychology of Reading*. Englewood Cliffs, NJ: Prentice-Hall.

References

Rumelhart, D. E. 1977. Toward an integrated model of reading. In Dominic S. (ed.) *Attention and Performance IV*. Hillsdale, NJ: Lawrence Erlbaum.

Rumelhart, D. E. 1984. Understanding Understanding. In James Flood (ed.) *Understanding Reading Comprehension*. Newark, Delaware: International Reading Research Association.

Rumelhart, D. E. *et al.* 1986. Schemata and sequential thought processes in PDP models. In McClelland and Rumelhart, 1986 op. cit.

Sarig, G. 1987. High-level reading in the first and foreign language: some comparative process data. In Devine *et al.* (eds.) *Research in Reading English as a Second Language*. Rowley, Mass.: Newbury House.

Sarig, G. ms. Comprehension-promotion strategies: the sum of the parts and the whole. Paper presented at the Second International Congress of Applied Psycholinguistics. University of Kassel 1988.

Scott, M. 1986. The understanding to direct: *conscientizacao* and reading. Working paper no. 18, CEPRIL. Sao Paulo: Universidad de Sao Paulo, Brazil.

Scott, M. 1990. *Demystifying the Jabberwocky: a Research Narrative*. Unpublished Ph.D. thesis, University of Lancaster.

Sheldon, S. A. 1984. Comparison of two teaching methods for reading comprehension. *Journal of Research in Reading*, 7, 1, 41–52.

Singer, H. and R. B. Ruddell (eds.) 1985. *Theoretical Models and Processes of Reading*. Third edition, Newark, Delaware: International Reading Research Association.

Smith, F. 1971. *Understanding Reading: A Psycholinguistic Analysis of Reading and Learning to Read*. New York: Holt Rinehart Winston.

Smith, F. 1973. *Psycholinguistics and Reading*. New York: Holt Rinehart Winston.

Southgate V. and H. Arnold. 1981. *Extending Beginning Reading*. London: Heinemann.

Stanovich, K. E. 1980. Toward an interactive-compensatory model of individual differences in the development of reading fluency. *Reading Research Quarterly*, 16, 32–71.

Swales, J. Aspects of article introductions. Ashton Research Report, no. 1. University of Ashton.

Swales, J. 1990. *Genre Analysis: English in Academic and Research Settings*. Cambridge: Cambridge University Press.

Taylor, M. 1990. Books in the classroom and knowledge about language. In Carter (ed.) *Knowledge About Language and the Curriculum: The LINC Reader*. London: Hodder and Stoughton.

Taylor, W. L. 1953. Cloze Procedure: a new tool for measuring readability, *Journalism Quarterly, Fall*, 415–433.

Thorndyke, P. W. 1977. Cognitive structures in comprehension and memory. *Cognitive Psychology*, 9, 1, 77–110.

Ulijn, J. M. and A. K. Pugh (eds.) 1985. *Reading for Professional Purposes: Methods and Materials in Teaching Languages*. Leuven: ACCO Contrastive Analysis Series.

Weber, R. 1970. First-graders' use of grammatical context in reading. In H. Levin and P. Williams (eds.) *Basic Studies on Reading*. New York: Basic Books.

Whitehead, F., A. C. Capey, W. Maddren and A. Wellings. 1977. *Children and Their Books*. London: Macmillan MEP.

Vauras, M., J. Hyonna and P. Niemi. 1992. Comprehending coherent and incoherent texts: evidence from eye movement and recall performance. *Journal of Research in Reading*, 15, 1, 39–53.

Wallace, C. 1992. *A Scheme for Teacher Education: Reading*. Oxford: Oxford University Press.

Index